# NAPOLEON

# NAPOLEON

Leslie McGuire

**1986**
**CHELSEA HOUSE PUBLISHERS**
**NEW YORK**
**NEW HAVEN   PHILADELPHIA**

SENIOR EDITOR: William P. Hansen
ASSOCIATE EDITORS: John Haney
                   Joy Johannessen
                   Richard Mandell
EDITORIAL COORDINATOR: Karyn Gullen Browne
EDITORIAL STAFF: Perry Scott King
ART DIRECTOR: Susan Lusk
LAYOUT: Irene Friedman
ART ASSISTANTS: Ghila Krajzman
                Carol McDougall
                Tenaz Mehta
COVER DESIGN: Robin Peterson
PICTURE RESEARCH: Ellen Cibula
                  Juliette Dickstein

First Printing

Library of Congress Cataloging in Publication Data

McGuire, Leslie. NAPOLEON

(World Leaders Past & Present)
Bibliography: p.
Includes index

    1. Napoleon I, Emperor of the French, 1769–1821—
Juvenile literature.   2. France—History—1789–1815—
Juvenile literature.   3. France—Kings and rulers—
Biography—Juvenile literature.   4. Generals—France—
Biography—Juvenile literature. [1. Napoleon I,
Emperor of the French, 1769–1821.   2. Kings, queens,
rulers, etc.   3. Generals.   4. France—History—1789–
1815]  I. Title.  II. Series.
DC203.M48   1986     944.05'092'4 [B] [92]   85—17170
ISBN 0-87754-554-5

**Chelsea House Publishers**

Harold Steinberg, Chairman & Publisher
Susan Lusk, Vice President
A Division of Chelsea House Educational Communications, Inc.

Chelsea House Publishers
133 Christopher Street
New York, N.Y. 10014

Pictures courtesy of The Bettmann Archive, Bibliothèque Nationale, An-
gers Fine Arts Museum, Musée de l'Armée, Musée Carnavalet, Musée du
Louvre, Musée National de Malmaison, Musée National de Versailles, The
New York Public Library, and the Prince Napoleon Collection, Paris

# Contents

# CHELSEA HOUSE PUBLISHERS

## WORLD LEADERS PAST & PRESENT

ADENAUER
ALEXANDER THE GREAT
MARK ANTONY
KING ARTHUR
KEMAL ATATÜRK
CLEMENT ATTLEE
BEGIN
BEN GURION
BISMARCK
LEON BLUM
BOLÍVAR
CESARE BORGIA
BRANDT
BREZHNEV
CAESAR
CALVIN
CASTRO
CATHERINE THE GREAT
CHARLEMAGNE
CHIANG KAI-SHEK
CHOU EN-LAI
CHURCHILL
CLEMENCEAU
CLEOPATRA
CORTEZ
CROMWELL
DANTON
DE GAULLE
DE VALERA
DISRAELI
EISENHOWER
ELEANOR OF AQUITAINE
QUEEN ELIZABETH I
FERDINAND AND ISABELLA

FRANCO
FREDERICK THE GREAT
INDIRA GANDHI
GANDHI
GARIBALDI
GENGHIS KHAN
GLADSTONE
HAMMARSKJÖLD
HENRY VIII
HENRY OF NAVARRE
HINDENBURG
HITLER
HO CHI MINH
KING HUSSEIN
IVAN THE TERRIBLE
ANDREW JACKSON
JEFFERSON
JOAN OF ARC
POPE JOHN XXIII
LYNDON JOHNSON
BENITO JUÁREZ
JFK
KENYATTA
KHOMEINI
KHRUSHCHEV
MARTIN LUTHER KING
KISSINGER
LENIN
LINCOLN
LLOYD GEORGE
LOUIS XIV
LUTHER
JUDAS MACCABEUS

MAO
MARY, QUEEN OF SCOTS
GOLDA MEIR
METTERNICH
MUSSOLINI
NAPOLEON
NASSER
NEHRU
NERO
NICHOLAS II
NIXON
NKRUMAH
PERICLES
PERÓN
QADDAFI
ROBESPIERRE
ELEANOR ROOSEVELT
FDR
THEODORE ROOSEVELT
SADAT
SUN YAT-SEN
STALIN
TAMERLAINE
THATCHER
TITO
TROTSKY
TRUDEAU
TRUMAN
QUEEN VICTORIA
WASHINGTON
CHAIM WEIZMANN
WOODROW WILSON
XERXES

*Further titles in preparation*

# ON LEADERSHIP
## Arthur M. Schlesinger, jr.

LEADERSHIP, it may be said, is really what makes the world go round. Love no doubt smooths the passage; but love is a private transaction between consenting adults. Leadership is a public transaction with history. The idea of leadership affirms the capacity of individuals to move, inspire and mobilize masses of people so that they act together in pursuit of an end. Sometimes leadership serves good purposes, sometimes bad; but whether the end is benign or evil, great leaders are those men and women who leave their personal stamp on history.

Now, the very concept of leadership implies the proposition that individuals can make a difference. This proposition has never been universally accepted. From classical times to the present day, eminent thinkers have regarded individuals as no more than the agents and pawns of larger forces, whether the gods and goddesses of the ancient world or, in the modern era, race, class, nation, the dialectic, the will of the people, the spirit of the times, history itself. Against such forces, the individual dwindles into insignificance.

So contends the thesis of historical determinism. Tolstoy's great novel *War and Peace* offers a famous statement of the case. Why, Tolstoy asked, did millions of men in the Napoleonic wars, denying their human feelings and their common sense, move back and forth across Europe slaughtering their fellows? "The war," Tolstoy answered, "was bound to happen simply because it was bound to happen." All prior history predetermined it. As for leaders, they, Tolstoy said, "are but the labels that serve to give a name to an end and, like labels, they have the least possible connection with the event." The greater the leader, "the more conspicuous the inevitability and the predestination of every act he commits." The leader, said Tolstoy, is "the slave of history."

Determinism takes many forms. Marxism is the determinism of class, Nazism the determinism of race. But the idea of men and women as the slaves of history runs athwart the deepest human instincts. Rigid determinism abolishes the idea of human freedom—the assumption of free choice that underlies every move we make, every word we speak, every thought we think. It abolishes the idea of human responsibility, since it is manifestly unfair to reward or punish people for actions that are by definition beyond their control. No one can live consistently by any deterministic

7

creed. The Marxist states prove this themselves by their extreme susceptibility to the cult of leadership.

More than that, history refutes the idea that individuals make no difference. In December 1931 a British politician crossing Park Avenue in New York City between 76th and 77th Streets around ten-thirty at night looked in the wrong direction and was knocked down by an automobile—a moment, he later recalled, of a man aghast, a world aglare: "I do not understand why I was not broken like an eggshell or squashed like a gooseberry." Fourteen months later an American politician, sitting in an open car in Miami, Florida, was fired on by an assassin; the man beside him was hit. Those who believe that individuals make no difference to history might well ponder whether the next two decades would have been the same had Mario Contasini's car killed Winston Churchill in 1931 and Giuseppe Zangara's bullet killed Franklin Roosevelt in 1933. Suppose, in addition, that Adolf Hitler had been killed in the street fighting during the Munich *Putsch* of 1923 and that Lenin had died of typhus during the First World War. What would the 20th century be like now?

For better or for worse, individuals do make a difference. "The notion that a people can run itself and its affairs anonymously," wrote the philosopher William James, "is now well known to be the silliest of absurdities. Mankind does nothing save through initiatives on the part of inventors, great or small, and imitation by the rest of us—these are the sole factors in human progress. Individuals of genius show the way, and set the patterns, which common people then adopt and follow."

Leadership, James suggests, means leadership in thought as well as in action. In the long run, leaders in thought may well make the greater difference to the world. But, as Woodrow Wilson once said, "Those only are leaders of men, in the general eye, who lead in action. . . . It is at their hands that new thought gets its translation into the crude language of deeds." Leaders in thought often invent in solitude and obscurity, leaving to later generations the tasks of imitation. Leaders in action—the leaders portrayed in this series— have to be effective in their own time.

And they cannot be effective by themselves. They must act in response to the rhythms of their age. Their genius must be adapted, in a phrase of William James's, "to the receptivities of the moment." Leaders are useless without followers. "There goes the mob," said the French politician hearing a clamor in the streets. "I am their leader. I must follow them." Great leaders turn the inchoate emotions of the mob to purposes of their own. They seize on the opportunities of their time, the hopes, fears, frustrations, crises, potentialities.

They succeed when events have prepared the way for them, when the community is waiting to be aroused, when they can provide the clarifying and organizing ideas. Leadership ignites the circuit between the individual and the mass and thereby alters history.

It may alter history for better or for worse. Leaders have been responsible for the most extravagant follies and most monstrous crimes that have beset suffering humanity. They have also been vital in such gains as humanity has made in individual freedom, religious and racial tolerance, social justice and respect for human rights.

There is no sure way to tell in advance who is going to lead for good and who for evil. But a glance at the gallery of men and women in *World Leaders—Past and Present* suggests some useful tests.

One test is this: do leaders lead by force or by persuasion? By command or by consent? Through most of history leadership was exercised by the divine right of authority. The duty of followers was to defer and to obey. "Theirs not to reason why,/ Theirs but to do and die." On occasion, as with the so-called "enlightened despots" of the 18th century in Europe, absolutist leadership was animated by humane purposes. More often, absolutism nourished the passion for domination, land, gold and conquest and resulted in tyranny.

The great revolution of modern times has been the revolution of equality. The idea that all people should be equal in their legal condition has undermined the old structures of authority, hierarchy and deference. The revolution of equality has had two contrary effects on the nature of leadership. For equality, as Alexis de Tocqueville pointed out in his great study *Democracy in America*, might mean equality in servitude as well as equality in freedom.

"I know of only two methods of establishing equality in the political world," Tocqueville wrote. "Rights must be given to every citizen, or none at all to anyone . . . save one, who is the master of all." There was no middle ground "between the sovereignty of all and the absolute power of one man." In his astonishing prediction of 20th-century totalitarian dictatorship, Tocqueville explained how the revolution of equality could lead to the "*Führerprinzip*" and more terrible absolutism than the world had ever known.

But when rights are given to every citizen and the sovereignty of all is established, the problem of leadership takes a new form, becomes more exacting than ever before. It is easy to issue commands and enforce them by the rope and the stake, the concentration camp and the *gulag*. It is much harder to use argument and achievement to overcome opposition and win consent. The Founding Fathers of the United States understood the difficulty. They believed that history had given them the opportunity to decide, as

Alexander Hamilton wrote in the first Federalist Paper, whether men are indeed capable of basing government on "reflection and choice, or whether they are forever destined to depend . . . on accident and force."

Government by reflection and choice called for a new style of leadership and a new quality of followership. It required leaders to be responsive to popular concerns, and it required followers to be active and informed participants in the process. Democracy does not eliminate emotion from politics; sometimes it fosters demagoguery; but it is confident that, as the greatest of democratic leaders put it, you cannot fool all of the people all of the time. It measures leadership by results and retires those who overreach or falter or fail.

It is true that in the long run despots are measured by results too. But they can postpone the day of judgment, sometimes indefinitely, and in the meantime they can do infinite harm. It is also true that democracy is no guarantee of virtue and intelligence in government, for the voice of the people is not necessarily the voice of God. But democracy, by assuring the rights of opposition, offers built-in resistance to the evils inherent in absolutism. As the theologian Reinhold Niebuhr summed it up, "Man's capacity for justice makes democracy possible, but man's inclination to injustice makes democracy necessary."

A second test for leadership is the end for which power is sought. When leaders have as their goal the supremacy of a master race or the promotion of totalitarian revolution or the acquisition and exploitation of colonies or the protection of greed and privilege or the preservation of personal power, it is likely that their leadership will do little to advance the cause of humanity. When their goal is the abolition of slavery, the liberation of women, the enlargement of opportunity for the poor and powerless, the extension of equal rights to racial minorities, the defense of the freedoms of expression and opposition, it is likely that their leadership will increase the sum of human liberty and welfare.

Leaders have done great harm to the world. They have also conferred great benefits. You will find both sorts in this series. Even "good" leaders must be regarded with a certain wariness. Leaders are not demigods; they put on their trousers one leg after another just like ordinary mortals. No leader is infallible, and every leader needs to be reminded of this at regular intervals. Irreverence irritates leaders but is their salvation. Unquestioning submission corrupts leaders and demeans followers. Making a cult of a leader is always a mistake. Fortunately hero worship generates its own antidote. "Every hero," said Emerson, "becomes a bore at last."

The signal benefit the great leaders confer is to embolden the rest of us to live according to our own best selves, to be active, insistent, and resolute in affirming our own sense of things. For great leaders attest to the reality of human freedom against the supposed inevitabilities of history. And they attest to the wisdom and power that may lie within the most unlikely of us, which is why Abraham Lincoln remains the supreme example of great leadership. A great leader, said Emerson, exhibits new possibilities to all humanity. "We feed on genius. . . . Great men exist that there may be greater men."

Great leaders, in short, justify themselves by emancipating and empowering their followers. So humanity struggles to master its destiny, remembering with Alexis de Tocqueville: "It is true that around every man a fatal circle is traced beyond which he cannot pass; but within the wide verge of that circle he is powerful and free; as it is with man, so with communities."

—New York

# 1

# The Eagle Hatches

The British fleet filled the harbor of Toulon, an important naval base in the south of France. Five surrounding ports, each boasting tremendous firepower, were teeming with British soldiers. The entire city, with its magnificent defense system, was firmly in the hands of the British.

It was August 1793. The French Revolution had begun four years earlier. The French people had overthrown King Louis XVI and proclaimed a republic, but they still had many problems.

When the king was beheaded in January 1793, his followers were horrified. Now many of them were revolting against the government in various parts of France. The other monarchies of Europe were also horrified. Britain, Holland, Spain, Austria and Prussia formed a coalition and made plans to attack France while it was disorganized and weakened by internal conflict.

In Toulon, royalist supporters of the guillotined king had called in the British to help them fight the revolutionary government, which had sent troops to lay siege to Toulon and recapture it. The French had a few cannon, not very well protected by poorly constructed earthworks. Their soldiers were untrained and short of supplies.

Twenty-four-year-old Captain Napoleon Bonaparte, on his way to a minor post on the Italian front, decided to make an unscheduled stop at Toulon to

Revolutionaries storm a nobleman's home in Paris in July 1789. The French Revolution brought sweeping social and political changes that helped pave the way for Napoleon's rise to power, though he himself did not actively participate in it.

Napoleon Bonaparte (1769–1821) at age 34, shortly before he became emperor of France. This famous portrait by François Gérard now hangs in the museum at Malmaison, where Napoleon spent much time with his wife and empress, Josephine (1763–1814).

13

Napoleon at age 22, two years before his dramatic success as an artillery commander at Toulon. He was, by all accounts, a rather shy, awkward, and opinionated young man who did not mix easily with his peers.

see a friend. As it happened, the officer in charge of the French artillery had been badly wounded, and Napoleon was offered the command. There began one of the most meteoric rises to fame and power the world has ever known.

Captain Bonaparte took over the artillery. After studying the situation, however, he realized that the entire siege was poorly organized. His cannon would be useless unless some major changes were made. He demanded to be put in charge, and because no one else seemed to know as much about artillery, his demand was granted.

Young Bonaparte moved the cannon to better positions and brought in food, horses, ammunition and guns. He trained his men, rebuilt his batteries, and then proceeded to direct all his firepower on the one weak spot in the enemy defenses. The British were pushed out of their strongest position, and a few days later Napoleon Bonaparte was promoted to the rank of major. After beating back a British attack, he was promoted to adjutant general.

Then, for five days, his cannon pounded the harbor while his troops took the forts, burned the British ships and armories, and finally stormed the gates of Toulon. By December Bonaparte was a brigadier general.

In four short months he had gone from captain to general—a very rapid rise. He was only 24, and because the rules said that a general had to be 25, he lied on the forms he filled out to get his commission. Although they recognized the brilliance of this courageous young officer, Napoleon Bonaparte's commanders were already uneasy about his ambition.

General Bonaparte's sallow face, with its high cheekbones, was framed by long black hair that looked as if it had never been combed. His uniform was much too big for him, hanging loosely on his five-foot-three frame. His crumpled boots were worn down at the heel and looked so large on his skinny legs that they seemed to belong to someone else. He spoke French with an odd accent. Who would ever have suspected that he would soon become

The French army captures Toulon from the British in December 1793. It was during the siege of Toulon that Napoleon's genius as a military strategist first became apparent to his superiors.

emperor of France and ruler of most of Europe? How was it possible?

Despite his appearance, Napoleon was brilliant and ambitious and could quickly change his plans to fit any new problem. But apart from his personal qualities, he had one other great advantage— he had the French Revolution behind him. The French Revolution was an extremely complex event, with many causes and effects. Basically, though, it started because the French peasants were tired of being starved and abused by their arrogant king, and because the rising middle class was tired of being excluded from power by the aristocracy. Only a few years before the siege of Toulon, the people decided to take their political fate into their own hands. In doing so, they unleashed forces that shaped the modern world.

The French Revolution led to the development of a much more powerful state than had ever existed before. This new state was more organized, more efficient, more centralized. The revolution brought the masses into the political process and touched every aspect of society. Because the revolutionaries believed they were making a clean break with the

**At the Battle of Hondschoo-
ten, in September 1793, an
Austrian army of 18,000
professional soldiers, confident of victory because of
their greater experience and
superior discipline, discovered that the recent events in
France had revolutionized
warfare as well as society. The
Austrians crumbled before
successive waves of poorly
trained but patriotic Frenchmen, who kept charging until
they prevailed, though they
sustained three times as many
casualties as the enemy.**

past, they even invented a new religion (whose ad-
herents worshipped an imaginary entity called the
"Supreme Being" and a new calendar, with 12 renamed months. For the first time, all French people became partners in nationhood.

The French Revolution also put an end to the old
style of gentlemanly warfare, as practiced by the
professional armies of the old kingdoms and monarchies. The revolutionary army was a popular army
fueled by patriotism. Not only that, by the end of
the 18th century many scientific advances had been
made. Roads were better, maps were better. Military theorists were teaching new principles involv-
ing massive troop concentrations and a new kind
of mobile warfare.

Napoleon appeared at a point in history when all
his talents could only send him to the top of this
new kind of state that was so well geared to a new
kind of warfare. Did Napoleon use the strong state
and the popular army to defend the revolution
against its many enemies? Or did he simply take
the forces created by the revolution and use them
for his own ends? More than 150 years after his
death, historians are still debating this question.

Napoleon Bonaparte was born on August 15,
1769, in Ajaccio, the capital of Corsica. A large
island in the Mediterranean, Corsica had long been
ruled by the Italian city-state of Genoa, and the
people spoke a dialect related to Italian. But in

Napoleon was born in this modest house in Ajaccio, Corsica, on August 15, 1769. His family was of Italian stock. He had to practice hard to learn to speak French without an Italian accent.

1768 Genoa had ceded Corsica to France. On the day of Napoleon's birth, the island was being forced to celebrate the first anniversary of the French takeover.

His father, Carlo Maria Buonaparte, was a lawyer. (Napoleon dropped the *u* from the spelling of his name after 1796, to make it more French.) Carlo and his wife, Letizia, though members of the petty nobility, were far from wealthy. Napoleon was the second of their eight children.

As a child Napoleon, or Nabulio, as he was then called, was small and puny. His oversized head often threw him off balance, and he had a terrible temper. Little Napoleon was always fighting with other boys.

A few years after Napoleon's birth, his father was appointed assessor of Ajaccio. Using this position, he managed to get a free education for his sons. At the age of 10, Napoleon was accepted at the military academy of Brienne, in northern France.

The little cadet was lonely and homesick in this school so far from home. All the other students belonged to the high aristocracy of France, and Napoleon was the son of a Corsican petty noble. He desperately wanted to learn correct French so they would not laugh at him. In this he was quite suc-

*We are members of a powerful monarchy, but today we feel only the vices of its constitution.*
—NAPOLEON BONAPARTE
writing in 1786

At the military academy of Brienne, France, where he was sent at age 10, Napoleon had a difficult time fitting in with his aristocratic fellow cadets, who teased him and appropriately nicknamed him "the Little Corporal."

Napoleon at age 16, when he was commissioned as a second lieutenant in the artillery. This sketch was drawn by one of his few friends at the royal military school in Paris.

cessful, but he never learned to spell. In addition, the handwriting of the future emperor was terrible. No one could read it—not even Napoleon. He was very good in mathematics, however, and since he did not have many friends at Brienne, he worked hard, sometimes studying all night.

Napoleon did well in his final exams and was accepted at the Ecole Militaire in Paris, the royal military school founded by King Louis XV. He had just turned 15 and was ecstatic.

Unfortunately, Napoleon continued to have similar problems in his new school. He was not well liked by his fellow students. They thought he was an uncivilized savage. Hurt by their insults, he became even more unsociable. He criticized everyone and everything around him, and even gave his teachers a difficult time. Nevertheless, Napoleon did fairly well in his studies. He read all the time, knew a great deal about history and geography, and was still outstanding in mathematics and the sciences. He was planning to join the navy.

But in 1785, when he was ready to graduate, examinations for the navy were canceled. Rather than stay in school for one more year, Napoleon decided to join the artillery. That September, at age 16, he was commissioned as a second lieutenant. He ranked 42nd out of the 56 students commissioned by Louis XVI that year.

Napoleon was sent to an artillery regiment at Valence, in southeastern France. His father had died while he was in school, and he was sending his small salary to his mother in Corsica. He stayed in Valence for six months and then took a long leave of absence to go back to Corsica and help his family.

After 22 months he returned to his regiment. He was assigned to a committee studying "the throwing of bombs with cannon." The youngest member of the committee, he astonished and impressed his commanding officers with his brilliant, detailed plans.

During those months the early rumblings of the French Revolution were heard in the land. By the time Napoleon rejoined his regiment in June 1788, unrest was already building. On July 14, 1789, a Paris mob stormed the Bastille prison, a hated symbol of tyranny. The revolutionaries took over the government, and although the king was still alive, his powers were limited.

Napoleon took no direct part in these events, but

**The storming of the Bastille, on July 14, 1789, marked the onset of the French Revolution. Napoleon returned to Corsica shortly after the outbreak of the revolution, hoping to play a role in the fight for Corsican independence.**

An angry revolutionary mob confronts King Louis XVI (at right, in the screened box; 1754–1793) after storming the Tuileries palace on August 10, 1792. In September the First Republic was proclaimed, and in January 1793 King Louis XVI was guillotined.

he was overjoyed to hear of the abolition of laws that kept petty nobles confined to the ranks. This meant that he no longer had to place any limits on his ambition. He could rise as high as he wished in the French army.

At first the revolution seemed to interest Napoleon mainly because it might enable him to play an important role in Corsica. He got another leave and returned to his homeland late in 1789, hoping to join forces with the Corsican revolutionary movement. Some time later he was posted to the Fourth Artillery regiment in France and promoted to first lieutenant. In September 1791, still feeling the pull of his native country, he obtained a three-month leave and returned home.

This time he forgot for a while that he was part of the French army. Napoleon became a lieutenant in the Corsican National Guard and took part in an attack on a fortress held by royalist French troops. He did not return to France when his leave was up, and in January 1792 he was charged with desertion.

Urged by his brother to go back to his regiment, Napoleon decided he had better go directly to Paris instead and plead his case with the minister of war. He arrived at the beginning of the tremendous upheavals that would bring the king to the guillotine and change the history of Europe.

As he wrote to his family: "This country is being torn apart by some very ferocious parties. It is hard to figure out what is going on among all the different factions. I do not know how things will turn out, but they will take a very revolutionary turn."

Napoleon managed to persuade the minister of war not only to send him back to his regiment without punishment but to make him a captain. He must have been fairly convincing to have avoided a court-martial for desertion. His new commission, signed "Louis" on July 30, 1792, was probably one of the last papers bearing the king's signature.

On August 10, 1792, Napoleon was in Paris when "the rabble" invaded the Tuileries palace and took the king prisoner. Napoleon is reported to have said that if he were king, he would never stand for such unruly behavior. It was this attack on the Tuileries that led to the establishment of a republic under a new government called the National Convention.

Two months later Napoleon again won permission to return to Corsica. By this time some of the Corsican revolutionaries had turned against France and were trying to break away from the revolutionary government in Paris. Napoleon opposed them and fought on the side of the Corsicans who remained loyal to France. In April 1793 Corsica plunged into civil war, and Napoleon left for France, taking the Bonaparte family with him.

During his seven and a half years in the French service, he had actually been on duty for only 30 months. He was still more attached to Corsica than to France. But by the time of his dramatic victory at Toulon, Napoleon had decided to tie his destiny to France.

> *In my family we kneel only to God.*
> —NAPOLEON BONAPARTE
> speaking during his
> days as a military cadet

Napoleon as a lieutenant colonel in the Corsican National Guard in 1791. Caught up in the revolutionary turmoil sweeping his homeland, Napoleon briefly deserted the French army but was reinstated and promoted to captain when France went to war with Austria.

# 2

# Shifting Fortunes

Once General Bonaparte had cast his lot with France, his rise to fame and fortune was swift. However, there were still some hard times ahead.

After his shining success at Toulon, Napoleon was assigned to France's Army of Italy as inspector of the coasts. He met a very pretty girl named Désirée Clary, who came from a wealthy family, and began to court her. At first, with his baggy uniform and long, messy hair, Napoleon made her laugh. Soon, though, Désirée fell under the spell of his flashing eyes, and they became engaged.

Her parents were outraged. After all, Napoleon Bonaparte was only a minor general. He would never be able to support their daughter in proper style! But the two young people were in love and stayed engaged in hopes that her parents would reconsider.

Meanwhile, Napoleon had a job to do. It took him to Nice, in the south of France, where he rented a small apartment in the home of Joseph Laurenti, a rich merchant. At this time he came to the attention of Maximilien Robespierre, who had risen to leadership of the National Convention after the execution of the king.

Revolutionary France during these years was not an easy country to govern. Not only was the Convention waging war with the revolution's enemies

Napoleon Bonaparte wearing the kind of ceremonial dress that was increasingly to appeal to him as his career took him closer to the center of political power in revolutionary France.

Napoleon's first great love, Désirée Clary, whose parents disapproved of the future French emperor because they thought he would never amount to much. However, they did allow Désirée's sister Julie to marry Napoleon's brother Joseph.

A contemporary engraving portraying Maximilien Robespierre (1758–1794), head of the Committee of Public Safety and patron of Napoleon, as the French Revolution's chief executioner.

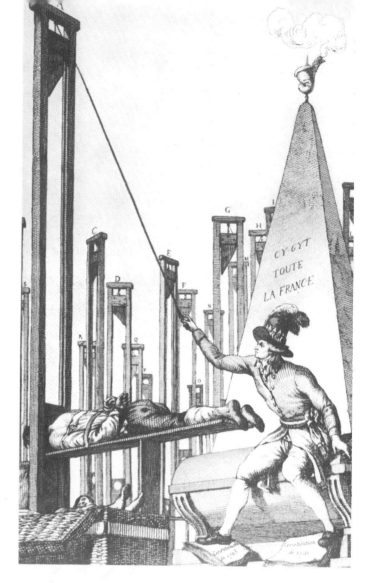

abroad, it was also locked in a bitter struggle to retain control at home. To deal with internal opposition, it had established a Committee of Public Safety with the power to execute anyone suspected of being an enemy of the revolution. As head of this committee, Robespierre was responsible for the deaths of some 50,000 people during the Reign of Terror.

Robespierre had heard about Napoleon's exploits at Toulon and considered him a true patriot. Napoleon had been working on a plan to cross the Alps and take Italy from the Austrians. Robespierre was enthusiastic about this plan, and it was soon accepted by the commanding general.

When Napoleon was not reading or working, he took long walks with young Emilie Laurenti. Though only 15, she soon helped Napoleon forget all about his fiancée, Désirée. He asked Madame Laurenti for Emilie's hand in marriage. Again he was turned down. What! Emilie marry some little raggedy soldier who was in the pay of those murderers in power in Paris? Especially when the pay was so little? Never!

The unhappy general suddenly forgot about Emilie and remembered his sweet Désirée. He wisely decided not to mention Emilie to her at all.

The execution of Robespierre, July 28, 1794. Ousted from the Committee of Public Safety, the man who had begun and supervised the Reign of Terror found himself condemned as excessively radical and facing the same guillotine to which he had sent so many political enemies.

Dispatched to Genoa on a mission, Napoleon thought his troubles were over. But on his return in July 1794, he found that his powerful protector, Robespierre, had been ousted and guillotined. Robespierre's initiation of a massive social revolution had earned him the hatred of the other members of the Convention, and they had moved against him, claiming that he had intended to make himself dictator. Now Napoleon too was under suspicion.

To his horror, the new, liberal French government (composed of Robespierre's political opponents) suspended him from his duties and arrested him. Napoleon was convinced that his career was over, if not his life. An investigation cleared him, and he was freed. But because of his ambition and his association with the radical members of the Convention, it took a long time before he was assigned to another post.

After the fall of Robespierre, the new government's troubles continued. It was still at war with foreign nations and the *émigrés*—royalists who had fled the country—were actively plotting to bring back the monarchy.

In addition, all over France there were uprisings like the one at Toulon. Some of the larger cities, such as Lyons, were in open rebellion. Certain regions that were far from Paris had joined the royalists, especially the Vendée. The peasants of this

**Napoleon in prison in Nice in 1794. Because of his association with Robespierre, Napoleon was jailed briefly on charges of conspiracy and treason. Had he been in Paris at the time, he probably would have been executed immediately.**

Revolutionaries fling royalist rebels from the parapets of a fortress in the Vendée, a region of France where the populace was in revolt against the new republican government. Napoleon had no stomach for what amounted to civil war and thus declined a post as commander of artillery in the Vendée.

largely Catholic agricultural part of western France had always had a good relationship with the nobility. When the French Revolution turned against the Roman Catholic church, they turned against the revolutionaries.

Much to Napoleon's disgust, when his post came through, he was assigned to the Vendée. This was a job he had no desire to take. He did not want to fight an army of poor people hiding in fields, hedges, and forests. He would have no use for artillery in such combat, and besides, fighting in a civil war would not bring the kind of fame he wanted.

Napoleon decided to leave for Paris immediately and explain his unhappiness to the minister of war in person. That method had worked well in the past. This time, however, he was not very successful. The minister of war thought his French so dreadful and his appearance so sloppy that Napoleon wound up with a vague job on the General Staff at half pay. Even this did not last.

In August he got a threatening letter demanding that he go to the Vendée or be replaced. Napoleon turned to the Committee of Public Safety. He again explained his plan to use the French Army of Italy

**Napoleon calls on Josephine de Beauharnais, widow of a nobleman who had been beheaded during the Reign of Terror. What began in 1795 as a courtship of convenience for both of them became a passionate romance.**

against Austria. The committee thought he was brilliant and assigned him to work on maps in the topographic bureau! That was almost as bad as the Vendée. He wanted to command men, to see action!

Napoleon began to cultivate his social life in hopes of meeting a powerful person who could help advance his career. It was during this period that he met Marie Josèphe Rose de Beauharnais, who would soon be his "incomparable Josephine."

Born in Martinique, she had married Viscount Alexandre de Beauharnais, who was beheaded during the Reign of Terror. She had two children, Hortense and Eugène. The pretty Creole widow, though no longer young, had all the grace and coquetry of the old regime. She herself had narrowly escaped the guillotine, so she was living life to the fullest in her search for a rich and powerful protector.

Napoleon forgot poor Désirée for good and fell hopelessly in love with Josephine, who stood for everything feminine and elegant. Even though Josephine did not think much of the young general, she flirted with him anyway, just as she did with many others, including General Paul Barras. Barras was an important member of the Convention who had helped to bring about Robespierre's downfall and had subsequently been appointed commander of Paris.

Meanwhile, revolutionary France remained in turmoil. Royalists at home and abroad continued to oppose the new regime, and the revolutionaries continued to quarrel among themselves. In 1795, in an attempt to consolidate power, the Convention drafted a new constitution that would establish a five-member ruling group called the Directory.

The royalists working to restore the monarchy realized that this new constitution would destroy their chances. Seizing arms, they fomented a revolt and marched on the Convention. There was fighting in the streets.

General Barras, who was a general in name only, realized he had no battle experience and needed a seasoned soldier to help. Having seen Napoleon in action during the siege of Toulon, Barras called upon him to take charge.

The next day, October 5, 1795, Napoleon fired into the rebel crowds with his artillery. Six hundred people were killed or wounded by what he later called "a whiff of grapeshot." Napoleon saved the Convention, and the new constitution went into effect. Five days later, on a motion by Barras, who was now commanding general of the Army of the Interior, Napoleon was appointed deputy commander.

When Barras became a Director—one of the five leaders of the new government—he resigned his military post. Unexpectedly, Napoleon Bonaparte succeeded him as commanding general of the Army of the Interior. Then, in March 1796, he was named commander in chief of the Army of Italy.

Paul Barras (1755–1829), the French revolutionary who led the coup against Robespierre in 1794. Impressed by Napoleon's performance at Toulon and wishing to advance the young general's career, Barras put him in command of the troops defending the National Convention.

On October 5, 1795 (13 Vendémiaire by the revolutionary calendar), royalist supporters took to the streets of Paris and stormed the Convention. In his first act, and one that gained him widespread attention, Napoleon dispersed the undermanned rebels with a "whiff of grapeshot," thus preventing the overthrow of the government.

This appointment was surprising, since little was known about Napoleon at the time except that he was a rather good artillery commander. But the promotion took place a week before Napoleon married Madame Josephine de Beauharnais. Some have suggested that the two events were connected.

Josephine had been under Barras' protection for some time, but she was an expensive lady who spent huge sums of money. Barras told her that Bonaparte had a very good future ahead of him. For his part, Napoleon thought Josephine was rich. Such was not the case. In any event, they agreed to marry.

They took their vows at the town hall on March 9, 1796, in a civil ceremony. On the marriage certificate, Napoleon wrote that he was two years older than he actually was, and Josephine took four years off her real age, 33.

Jean Baptiste Jules Bernadotte (1763–1844), a fellow officer and friend of Napoleon's, eventually married Désirée Clary, the woman Napoleon spurned. In 1810, with Napoleon's backing, he became crown prince of Sweden but shortly thereafter allied himself with Napoleon's enemies.

And what about Désirée? When she heard about Napoleon's marriage she swore that she would never wed and threatened suicide. A year and a half later, she married a young captain named Bernadotte. A friend of Napoleon and his brother Joseph, Bernadotte would later play an important role in Napoleon's life.

It is possible that Barras engineered Napoleon's marriage to Josephine and made him commander of the Army of Italy in return for taking the merry young widow—and her bills—off his hands. Then again, perhaps he thought Napoleon was gaining too much political power. As long as Napoleon was in France, he could be a threat. Barras may have promoted Napoleon so he could send him to Italy. That would certainly get him out of the political arena.

Less than six months later, Napoleon had such a dazzling string of military victories behind him that all of France, and even the rest of Europe, was amazed. Perhaps the most amazed of all was the man who had made it possible, Napoleon's sponsor, Barras.

# 3

# The Conquest of Italy

Shortly after his wedding day, Napoleon set out to take command of the Army of Italy. In a way, his campaign was intended less to give France power in Italy than to give the French a strong bargaining position to force concessions from Austria. Perhaps most important was the fact that the French government had no money. Napoleon was really asked to plunder and pillage Italy in order to fill the Directory's treasury.

It may seem strange that France hoped to strike at Austria by attacking Italy, but in the late 18th century the map of Europe looked very different than it looks today. Austria was not the relatively small nation it is now, but a large and powerful empire. Italy was not a unified country, but a collection of separate states. Some were independent, like the Papal States, the republics of Venice and Genoa, and the Kingdom of Sardinia; others belonged to foreign powers, primarily Austria, which claimed Milan, Mantua, Tuscany and Modena.

Germany was in a similar situation. The most powerful German state was Prussia; most of the others were weak and divided. The year before Napoleon's Italian campaign, Prussia had signed a treaty giving France the states on the left bank of the Rhine River, the part of Germany closest to France. But Austria refused to recognize this treaty and took up arms against France.

---

**Napoleon at the Battle of Arcola, one of the great victories that he gained in 1796 during his Italian campaign. This heroic work was painted by Antoine-Jean Gros (1771–1835), whom Napoleon commissioned to immortalize his exploits on canvas.**

*I am a soldier and accustomed to risking my life every day. I am full of the fire of youth; I cannot act with the restraint of an accomplished diplomat.*
—NAPOLEON BONAPARTE
to the Austrian ambassador, following the negotiation of the Treaty of Campo-Formio in 1797

**Archduke Charles of Austria, brother of the Holy Roman Emperor Francis II (1768–1835), was one of the more able Austrian generals that Napoleon faced during his Italian campaign.**

Napoleon on the road from Paris to Nice, headquarters of the French Army of Italy. He missed Josephine terribly and wrote her ardent love letters from every stop he made en route: "I feel passion strangling me. The day when I lose your heart, Nature will lose for me all her warmth and greenery."

The war in Germany was not going well for the French, so they hoped that success on the Italian front would give them leverage. With a series of victories in Italy, they might be able to pressure Austria into yielding the left bank of the Rhine.

Napoleon had no doubt that the plan he had thought up in 1794—the one that had so impressed Robespierre—would bring such victories. But the army with which he was supposed to carry out this plan was in terrible shape.

The Army of Italy had been sitting at the foot of the Alps for three years. One of its battalions refused to leave France until it had been paid. There was no food, no ammunition, and no money to buy any.

Napoleon set up his headquarters in Nice and received his generals. They took one look at their new commander—a short, skinny 26-year-old with long, messy hair, who held a portrait of his new wife in one hand and insisted that everyone look at it—and were not impressed. They thought he was a political schemer who had managed to get this post through back-room deals. Did he really expect to take on the Austrian Empire with 27,000 ragged, hungry soldiers who had not been paid in months and wore shoes made of straw?

But young Napoleon was not the least bit intimidated by them. He asked about the size of their units, troop morale, and supplies. Then he said he would inspect the soldiers the next day and begin to march the day after.

He was not quite on schedule, but he was not far off either. Within 48 hours he managed to get enough bread, meat, and brandy to last 6 days. He split up the soldiers in the rebellious battalion and spread them out among all the other units, thus diffusing their anger.

To give his troops a strong feeling of identity, he held a formal review. His speech to them shows his great ability to inspire courage in his men.

Napoleon in Italy, as sketched by Gros. Though short and habitually unkempt, Napoleon proved himself an inspiring leader of men. Within just days of taking command, he began to turn France's demoralized Army of Italy into a spirited fighting force.

"Soldiers, you are naked and undernourished. The government owes you much, but can give you nothing. . . . Your patience in bearing all privations and your courage in facing all kinds of danger have won the admiration of France. She is a witness to your hardships. You have no shoes or coats or shirts, and almost no food. Our supply depots are empty, while the enemy's are stuffed. It is up to you to capture them. You want to do it, and you can do it. Let's go!"

He electrified his soldiers and began his march on April 2, 1796. Instead of tackling the well-defended passes through the Alps, he quickly marched his army across Genoese territory. He beat back Austro-Sardinian forces in four battles, and on April 28 the king of Sardinia agreed to a truce. The Austrian army retreated to protect the city of Milan.

After these first victories, Napoleon made another speech to his troops.

"Soldiers! Up to this time you have fought for nothing better than barren rocks—which although made famous by your courage, are useless to the Fatherland. . . . Lacking everything, you have made up for everything you lacked. You have won battles without cannon, crossed rivers without bridges, made forced marches without boots, and bivouacked without brandy and often without bread. Only the soldiers of liberty could have endured what you have endured! For all this, my thanks."

Then, after requesting that they respect the civilian population, he continued: "You still have battles to fight, cities to take, and rivers to cross. You have done nothing, since you have everything to do. . . ."

When he signed the peace treaty with the king of Sardinia, he wrote into it the "right to cross the Po River at Valenza." The Austrian general was completely fooled and immediately took his troops off to Valenza to lie in wait for the French army.

But Napoleon calmly crossed the river at Piacenza instead, taking the Austrians by surprise from behind. After the Battle of Lodi, the rich province of Lombardy fell into his lap. Now Milan was wide

*General Bonaparte is not without defects. . . . Sometimes he is hard, impatient, abrupt or imperious. . . . He has not been respectful enough towards the Government commissioners. When I reproved him for this, he replied that he could not possibly treat otherwise men who were universally scorned for their immorality and incapacity.*

—HENRI CLARKE
senior French commander,
describing Napoleon's conduct
during the Italian campaign

open to his advance. Archduke Ferdinand of Austria left that city in a great hurry, taking with him his gold and art collections.

After each conquest, Napoleon presented himself as a liberator. Even though the Directors had told him not to help revolutionary movements in Italy—France did not want any Italian entanglements—Napoleon disobeyed. He addressed the Italians in stirring words.

"People of Italy! The French army comes to break your chains. The French nation is the friend of all nations; receive us with trust! Your property, your religion, your customs will be respected. We shall wage war like generous enemies, for our only quarrel is with the tyrants who have enslaved you."

The citizens of Milan greeted Napoleon with open arms and jubilation. He emptied their treasury and marched south. He conquered the Grand Duchy of Tuscany, the duchies of Modena and Parma, and the papal city-states of Bologna and Ferrara. This diversion took him a month and secured vast

On May 10, 1796, with Napoleon himself in the lead, the French army stormed the bridge over the Adda River in the face of fierce opposition and captured the city of Lodi, in northern Italy.

As Napoleon swept through Italy, he seized and had shipped to France many of the peninsula's great cultural treasures. Among them was this well-known bronze statue of four horses pulling a chariot that dated from Roman times and had adorned St. Mark's Church in Venice until his arrival.

amounts of money, horses, ammunition, food, and equipment. Napoleon also looted the great cultural treasures of these states, sending to France many priceless paintings and other works of art.

The Directory was delighted with the spoils but less ecstatic about the fact that Napoleon was negotiating all the treaties himself. He did not ask for their permission or their stamp of approval. His popularity was growing by leaps and bounds, and the Directors were in no position to stop him.

Throughout the entire campaign, the Austrian

generals in Italy made the mistake of dividing their troops, thus handing Napoleon some easy victories. He also had an advantage because his army was very different from the armies it faced. The Austrian troops were paid professional soldiers. They would continue to eat whether they won or lost. But for the French army, victory meant food and clothes. Defeat meant starvation.

Napoleon's only problem in Italy was Mantua. His troops tried for a month to bring the city to its knees, but Mantua refused to surrender. A fresh division of Austrian troops was sent to break the French army. Soon there were rumors in France that Napoleon was about to lose Italy.

But in January 1797 the Austrian general again made the fatal mistake. Although his army was much larger than Napoleon's, he split it into two groups. This made Napoleon's strategy simple. He attacked the left flank of the Austrian army and demolished it. The rest of the Austrian troops fled.

Napoleon enters Milan on May 14, 1796. The people happily greeted him as a liberator who would free them from Austrian rule.

In January 1797, at the Battle of Rivoli, Napoleon's horse was shot out from under him. Undeterred, he quickly remounted and led his troops to yet another major victory.

In hot pursuit, Napoleon set out across the Alps. When he was practically at the gates of Vienna, Austria's capital, the Austrians decided to negotiate. The result was the preliminary peace treaty of Leoben, signed in April 1797. Napoleon concluded this treaty on his own authority, without the approval of the Directors, who considered the terms too generous to Austria.

Although the Directors were not pleased with his personal diplomacy, they were anxious to keep Napoleon out of Paris. They thought he was growing far too popular with the French people and might be dangerous if he returned.

Whenever the Directors complained about his political maneuvers in Italy, Napoleon would remind them how much money his campaigns brought in and threaten to come home. Suddenly the weather was too hot for him, or he was feeling ill, or he had to rush to Paris to defend himself against charges that he was mishandling the campaign. By manipulating the Directors with such threats, he managed to win their agreement to every one of his plans. He knew how to turn his military success and his popularity into bases of political power.

Napoleon stayed in Italy to complete the peace negotiations, but the Austrians were in no hurry to reach a final agreement. Elections had recently been held in France, and the royalists had done well in the Council of Elders and the Council of Five Hundred (the two houses of the French parliament). Both councils were fighting with the Directors, the Directors were fighting with each other, and the Austrians were hoping for a royalist takeover of the government.

As the royalists became an increasing menace to the republic, the Directors decided they had no choice but to call upon Bonaparte and his army. Too weak and divided to turn to the French people for defense or to come up with a political solution, they wanted Napoleon to impose a military solution.

Napoleon was not the only general fighting for revolutionary France, but he was undoubtedly the most successful. In this drawing Napoleon (center), holding a map of the vast areas he conquered during the Italian campaign, appears distinctly unimpressed by the much less significant conquests of generals Louis Hoche (1768–1797), Jean Victor Moreau (1763–1813), and Charles Pichegru (1761–1804).

Pierre François Charles Augereau (1757–1816), one of Napoleon's most outstanding generals. While Napoleon was fighting in Italy, another royalist plot threatened the Directory in Paris. Augereau, dispatched by Napoleon to support the Directors, duly suppressed the insurrection on September 4, 1797 (18 Fructidor by the revolutionary calendar).

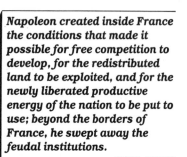

Napoleon created inside France the conditions that made it possible for free competition to develop, for the redistributed land to be exploited, and for the newly liberated productive energy of the nation to be put to use; beyond the borders of France, he swept away the feudal institutions.

—KARL MARX
German socialist philosopher

Napoleon had been alarmed by the election results and had urged the Directors to suppress the royalists. But when they actually sent for him, he played his cards carefully. If the coup against the royalists failed, he did not want to be too closely associated with it. So instead of going to Paris himself, he sent one of his generals, Pierre Augereau. Augereau arrived on August 7, and by September 4 the royalists had been defeated.

Napoleon claimed the victory as his own, and the Austrians suddenly decided to make a hasty final settlement. According to one story, while he was negotiating with the Austrian ambassador, Cobenzl, he accidentally knocked over a tray of plates. When they smashed on the floor, he is supposed to have said to Cobenzl, "I will break you in the same way."

The Treaty of Campo-Formio was signed on October 17, 1797. It basically confirmed the earlier Peace of Leoben, leaving Austria in control of important areas of Italy. But the French claimed the Low Countries (modern-day Belgium, Luxembourg, and the Netherlands) and much of Italy, and won a secret promise that Austria would yield the left bank of the Rhine to France.

Napoleon signed the treaty without authorization from the Directors, but the French people were delirious with joy. When he returned to Paris on December 5, a huge official celebration awaited him. The Directors realized that they could not afford to let the people know how irritated they were. They proclaimed that the treaty fulfilled all their wishes, and they immediately gave Napoleon command of the Army of England—anything to get him out of Paris.

The Directors knew the truth of the saying that there is nothing more dangerous than an unemployed hero.

Napoleon negotiates the Treaty of Campo-Formio in October 1797. In this painting by E. A. Guillon, he has just smashed a tray of crockery on the floor and is warning the startled Austrian ambassador (second from right) that his country stands to meet the same kind of treatment unless agreement is reached.

BONAPARTE

# 4

# Success in Everything

Napoleon was supposed to plan an invasion of England, but one look at the untrained troops gathered along the English Channel showed him that the idea was impractical. He suggested to the Directors that he invade Egypt and the island of Malta instead. With a foothold in the Mediterranean, Napoleon claimed, he could destroy England.

The entire Egyptian campaign was a disaster in the long run, but Napoleon never told the story quite that way. As far as the French people were concerned, Napoleon was still the great conquering hero. When news of his victories reached Paris—news Napoleon cleverly wrote himself—all things Egyptian became the latest fad.

He set out on May 19, 1798, with 300 ships crammed with 30,000 soldiers and 16,000 sailors. In addition, there were 167 members of a scientific and artistic commission, plus supplies for everyone. The news was no secret—it was reported in *The Times* of London.

Lord Nelson, the famous British admiral, immediately set sail after him, but Bonaparte's luck held. Nelson kept sailing right by, barely missing the French fleet as it made its lumbering way first to Malta and then to the Egyptian port of Alexandria. The Knights of Malta, a long-established chivalric order, gave in after three days, and the feeble forces in Alexandria collapsed even more quickly.

Named for the city in northern Egypt where Napoleon's troops found it in 1799, the Rosetta Stone enabled scholars to decipher the ancient Egyptian hieroglyphics for the first time.

---

***Napoleon Crossing the St. Bernard Pass***, by Jacques-Louis David (1748–1825), the most famous French painter of Napoleon's time. Napoleon later named him First Painter of the Empire.

Admiral Horatio Nelson (1758–1805), commander of the British fleet that attempted to intercept Napoleon Bonaparte on his way to Egypt.

At the time, Egypt was officially under Turkish control but was actually run by the Mamelukes. *Mameluke* means "bought man" in Arabic. Originally slaves, the Mamelukes were used as warriors by Egypt's rulers and eventually managed to become the rulers themselves. As he had done in Italy, Napoleon entered Alexandria as the great liberator. He told the Egyptians that he would respect their beliefs and deliver them from Mameluke tyranny:

"Peoples of Egypt, you will be told that I have come to destroy your religion. Do not believe it! Reply that I have come to restore your rights and to punish the usurpers, and that I respect God, his prophet, and the Koran more than the Mamelukes do. . . . What wisdom, what talents, what virtues distinguish the Mamelukes, so that they have exclusive possession of everything that makes life sweet and enjoyable? Is there a beautiful slave girl, a fine horse, a handsome house? Those things, too, belong to the Mamelukes. If Egypt is their farm, let them show us the lease that God gave them on it."

Then Napoleon and his army began the terrible march across the desert to Cairo, Egypt's capital. Their enemies were not so much the Mamelukes as heat, thirst, and lack of supplies. Although brave and fierce, the Mamelukes were completely disorganized. Despite the loss of many soldiers in the desert, Napoleon defeated a large Mameluke force in the Battle of the Pyramids and took Cairo easily.

Shortly after the victory at Cairo, Napoleon's Egyptian campaign was derailed by Admiral Nelson. He finally caught up with the French fleet at Aboukir Bay and destroyed it completely. Napoleon was now cut off from France, his dreams of humbling Britain scuttled along with the fleet.

Marooned in Cairo, he made good use of his time. He immediately put his scientists and administrators to work. They set up new systems to reorganize everything from land surveys, taxation, and hospitals to street lights and garbage removal. They even built French-style cafes. Nevertheless, Napoleon's power in Egypt rested on shaky ground. Despite his fine speeches, the Egyptians consid-

*Soldiers, consider that from the summit of these pyramids, forty centuries look down upon you.*
—NAPOLEON BONAPARTE
speaking to his troops in 1798, shortly before the Battle of the Pyramids

**Napoleon (left) oversees the departure of the French expedition to Egypt, May 19, 1798. The logistics of transporting large armies over great expanses of land or water never daunted Napoleon.**

ered the French forces an army of occupation, not liberation.

Napoleon soon ran out of money. The heavy taxes that he forced upon the Egyptians (much to their anger and resentment) were nevertheless insufficient for his purposes. His troops went unpaid, and food and materials were always in short supply. Many soldiers had syphilis and other diseases. In December bubonic plague struck, and more men died every day. But in his report to the Directors, Napoleon said, "We lack nothing here. We are bursting with strength, good health and high spirits."

And indeed the situation was not entirely without useful results. The scientific commission was busy investigating every aspect of Egyptian life and history. Up until then most information about this huge and fascinating country came from stories by travelers and ancient writers like Herodotus. Napoleon's scientists studied mummified cats and birds, the wildlife of the Nile River, and Oriental music. They made good maps of the area, explored the

**The Battle of the Pyramids, July 24, 1798. In this stylized woodcut, French soldiers backed by 50 cannon brace themselves to withstand a charge by fierce Mameluke cavalrymen.**

ancient ruins, and did archaeological research.

One of the most important results of Bonaparte's Egyptian campaign was the discovery of the Rosetta Stone, a slab of rock inscribed in Greek and hieroglyphics. Hieroglyphics were the writing symbols of the ancient Egyptian language, but their meaning was a mystery. In 1821 a French scholar named Champollion used the Rosetta Stone to decipher the hieroglyphics. Champollion was nine years old when Napoleon's engineers first found the Stone.

Napoleon also made detailed plans for a canal at the town of Suez that would connect the Red Sea to the Mediterranean. Although he was never able to build it, his dream was realized when the French began construction of the present Suez Canal in 1859.

In February 1799 Napoleon decided to march into Syria. It was a disastrous move, and he suffered a terrible defeat by the Turks and their British allies at the fortress of Acre. In his reports, however, he claimed to have destroyed the town.

Admiral Nelson routs the French at the Battle of the Nile, in a cartoon by British caricaturist James Gillray (1757–1815). The caption reads: "Extirpation of the Plagues of Egypt;—Death of the Revolutionary Crocodiles;—or, the British Hero cleansing the Mouth of the Nile."

*Unavoidable wars are always just.*
—NAPOLEON BONAPARTE
speaking shortly after the Battle of Marengo in 1800

**Napoleon inspects a mummy discovered by his team of scientific and archaeological experts. He was interested in Egypt's culture and history as well as its strategic value in the war against Great Britain.**

Retreating to Cairo, Napoleon received word in July that the Turks were landing at Alexandria. Fortunately for the plague-infested, exhausted French troops, the Turkish forces were small and their attack disorganized. This time the French were victorious.

After the battle, Napoleon saw a copy of a French newspaper found aboard one of the British ships that had come with the Turks. It carried bad news from home. Austria, Russia, Britain, and Turkey had formed the Second Coalition, which had defeated French troops in Italy and attacked Switzerland and Germany. What was worse, inside France itself the royalists were in control of many western provinces, and the Directory was bankrupt and politically unstable.

Napoleon decided then and there to ignore his orders and return to France. He later discovered, however, that in leaving Egypt he actually was obeying orders. The frightened Directors had sent instructions for him to sail for France at once, but he had not yet received them.

At 5:00 A.M. on August 22, 1799, Napoleon deserted his army and his command, sneaking out of Egypt with five of his generals and two of the scientists.

By the time Napoleon returned to France, one

member of the Directory, Emmanuel Sieyès, had already decided that the government should be reorganized. Sieyès wanted to limit the power of the elected parliament and make the Directory a great deal stronger. What he really wanted was a *coup d'état*, a takeover, supported by the army, and he needed a general to pull it off. But which of the generals could he trust?

When Napoleon arrived in Paris, the people greeted him as the one man who could save the Republic of France. Sieyés was not so sure, but he finally decided that he could handle Napoleon. Once he was in power, he would buy Napoleon off with a minor role in the coup and then quietly send him back to Egypt or some other equally remote location.

A variety of diseases, including a particularly deadly outbreak of the plague, ravaged the French army during the Egyptian expedition. In March 1799 Napoleon visited the hospital at Jaffa to show his concern for his soldiers and to improve their morale.

Priest - turned - revolutionary Emmanuel Sieyès (1748–1836). A very skillful, opportunistic politician, he conspired with Napoleon to overthrow the Directory in the *coup d'état* (takeover of state) of 18 Brumaire (November 9, 1799). Though a Director himself, Sieyès thought he could use Napoleon to get rid of his rivals and thus emerge as the most powerful figure in the new government.

Napoleon knew an opportunity when he saw one. He agreed to help, and the plans were made. Among the supporters of the coup were the French Foreign Minister Talleyrand and Napoleon's brother Lucien, who was president of the Council of Five Hundred (the lower house of parliament).

On November 9, 1799, the Council of Elders (the upper house) voted to send the entire parliament to the palace of Saint-Cloud in the countryside near Paris. Using the excuse that there was a terrorist plot to overthrow the government, they made Bonaparte commander in chief of all the Paris troops. They claimed they were removing the parliament for its own safety.

The decree of November 9 was approved with ease—owing to the fact that notices of the 8:00 A.M. vote were delivered at 5:00 A.M., and only to the members who were in on the plot. According to the revolutionary calendar, November 9 was 18 Brumaire, or the 18th day of the "month of mists." Thus this episode in French history is known as the coup d'état of 18 Brumaire.

The next day, 19 Brumaire (November 10), the entire parliament met at Saint-Cloud. By this time, the opposition had learned of the plot and was there in force. They angrily demanded to know why parliament was meeting outside Paris, surrounded by the army. Shouting "Down with dictators!" and "Down with the tyrant!" the toga-clad members crowded to the front of the room and attacked Napoleon.

The man who was fearless in the face of armed enemies completely lost his nerve. He had to be rescued by one of his generals. Once outside, pale and shaking, he was unable to do anything but stammer, "They wanted to kill me; they wanted to outlaw me."

Napoleon's brother Lucien could not restore order, so he went to get the legislative guards who were supposed to protect the parliament. He convinced them that a small group of raving lunatics was inside threatening to kill the Five Hundred. The guards set their bayonets and rushed in to save their representatives.

On seeing the bayonets, the confused legislators fled through the windows with their togas flapping and disappeared into the bushes. A few hours later, the frightened parliament met again and voted in a new three-member executive to replace the Directory. It was called the Consulate, and it was composed of Sieyès, Napoleon, and a third man named Roger Ducos.

During the next few weeks, the Consuls drafted a new constitution. Sieyès did most of the work, and Napoleon reaped most of the rewards—after all, he was head of the army. After Napoleon made a simple remark about how they would find themselves up to their knees in blood if he failed to get

**Napoleon (center) on the morning of 18 Brumaire, conferring with his family and supporters (from left to right): Jean Bernadotte (1763–1844) and Napoleon's brother Joseph (1768–1844); Josephine; her children, Hortense and Eugène de Beauharnais (behind their mother); Napoleon's brother Lucien (1775–1840); his brother-in-law Joachim Murat (1767–1815); (partially obscured) his chief of staff, Louis Berthier (1753–1815); and Charles Talleyrand (1754–1838), later his foreign minister (leaning against the chair).**

**Panic in the Council of Five Hundred. After being rescued from the angry legislators by his brother Lucien, Napoleon returned to the council chamber with armed guards who frightened them out of their wits (and, in some cases, out of the windows). Shortly thereafter they agreed to do away with the Directory and launch the Consulate.**

> *Being in the Tuileries is not everything: what matters is to stay here.*
> —NAPOLEON BONAPARTE
> on becoming First Consul and taking up residence in the Tuileries palace

his way, the other two Consuls decided not to make trouble. Napoleon was named First Consul for a term of 10 years.

On February 7, 1800, the Consulate held a plebiscite, or national vote, on the Constitution of the Year VIII. (The revolutionary calendar began in 1792, the year of the proclamation of the republic, so 1800 was the Year VIII.) More than 3 million people voted in favor of Napoleon and the new constitution; only 1,500 voted against it. The other two Consuls had very little power, and Napoleon, at age 30, had France in the palm of his hand.

He moved into the old royal palace of the Tuileries and proceeded to reorganize the French government and fill the empty treasury. He also mapped out a plan to defeat Austria once and for all, while making sure French possessions in Germany, Switzerland, and Italy were secure.

In a bold move, he took 22,000 men across the Alps. Fighting snow, ice, avalanches, and winds, he marched horses, troops, and supply sleds across the Great St. Bernard pass into northern Italy. Finally, exhausted, hungry, and frozen, his army arrived at Marengo. He had been planning to take the Austrians by surprise, but 35,000 Austrian troops took him by surprise instead.

Napoleon had sent one of his divisions, commanded by General Desaix, on another mission. Now his badly outnumbered men were taking a beating from the Austrians. By the afternoon of June 14, 1800, it looked as if Napoleon had lost the Battle of Marengo in a sea of mud.

Then, miraculously, Desaix appeared with his 5,000 men. "It is three o'clock," he said. "The battle is lost. But we have time to win another."

The Austrians, who thought the fighting was over, were completely unprepared for the renewed French attack. They fled, and the Battle of Marengo became a last-minute French victory for Napoleon.

Not only was Marengo a military victory that broke up the Second Coalition, it was a political victory as well. If Napoleon had been defeated there—as he almost was—his life, and the course of history, might have been very different.

Napoleon was threatened and denounced as a dictator when he proclaimed the dissolution of the Directory at the Council of Five Hundred in Saint-Cloud in November 1799.

# 5

# From First Consul to Emperor

As First Consul, Napoleon took the reins of the French government into his own hands. His experience in governing Egypt and Italy was a great help, and Napoleon was a man of enormous energy. He once said, "All great events hang by a single thread. The clever man takes advantage of everything, neglects nothing that may give him some added opportunity." That was how he had become First Consul, and he continued to take advantage of every opportunity, even when it looked as if he had already reached the peak of his career.

Sieyès had wanted the job of First Consul to be symbolic, with no real power. But Napoleon had the army and the love of the French people, and he used them to take complete control. He announced that the revolution was now complete and peace had come at long last. He claimed he would heal the old wounds, and he worked hard to restore the appearance of harmony.

He invited back the *émigrés*—all the royalists and others who were considered enemies of the revolution and had left France. He wanted the French people to feel united, to be one country again after years of fighting and division.

---

Napoleon liked to think of himself as the reincarnation of great rulers of the past—Charlemagne, Alexander the Great, Julius Caesar. His grandiose visions were echoed in many contemporary paintings such as Ingres's *Apotheosis of Napoleon*, in which the laurel-wreathed emperor ascends to heaven in a Roman chariot.

A letter from Napoleon to the count of Provence, dated September 1800. As First Consul, Napoleon extended amnesty to most of the royalist *emigrés* (exiles) who had fled France, with the exception of extreme reactionaries like the count. "You ought not to wish to return to France," Napoleon wrote. "You would have to walk over 100,000 corpses."

Napoleon and Pope Pius VII (1742–1823) sign the Concordat of 1801. Revolutionary France and the Catholic church had been at odds since 1789, but with this agreement the pope recognized the revolution, and Napoleon recognized the Church.

Napoleon also decided that France should resume relations with the Catholic church. During the monarchy, the Church had owned tremendous amounts of land and was very wealthy. The new republic had seized the Church's land and given it to the people. Pope Pius VI had condemned the revolution and its principles, and there had been a break with the Church.

Though Napoleon himself did not care about religion, he realized how useful it was to society. He also realized that a great many French people had not abandoned their faith. To end the religious turmoil caused by the revolution, Napoleon began negotiations with the new pope, Pius VII. After months of talks, they signed an agreement called the Concordat of 1801.

The Concordat established religious freedom while recognizing Catholicism as the main religion of France and binding the state to pay the salaries of the clergy. In exchange, the pope recognized the republic and gave up all claim to Church property seized during the revolution.

With the Concordat, Napoleon removed one of the main arguments against the new regime from the royalist opposition. Now the royalists could no longer use the issue of religion to win support from the peasants.

Napoleon set up the Council of State at the head of his government. He sat in on all the sessions and used it to run the entire country. He met personally with each minister, read all the reports, took part in all the debates, and countersigned all the decisions.

In reorganizing the government, Napoleon finished the job begun by the revolution. He abolished the old authorities and divided the country into 98 administrative units called departments. This system, which still exists today, gave the central government more control, increased efficiency, and contributed to a feeling of national unity.

Napoleon also stabilized the finances of France. The treasury was full once more, and he kept a close watch on where the money went. Members of the government were no longer free to dip into the treasury, as they seemed to have done during the Directory. He created the Bank of France and did not allow the discrimination and corruption that had been a way of life during the monarchy.

As soon as he took power, Napoleon put a group of lawyers to work to reform the legal system. They took the large, conflicting jumble of old laws and codes that had been handed down over hundreds of years and turned them into a clear set of laws in plain language. This Civil Code was later called the Napoleonic Code. Carried all over Europe by his armies, it laid the foundation for most modern European legal codes.

Napoleon wanted to make Paris the most beautiful city in the world as well as the center of government. The Louvre, a great art museum, was already full of the treasures he had sent back from the first

> *Clever policy consists in making nations believe they are free.*
> —NAPOLEON BONAPARTE
> on becoming First Consul for life

Napoleon consults with artisans working on the facade of the Louvre, France's greatest art museum. His Italian campaign had added many masterpieces to its fine collections, and after he became emperor it was renamed Musée Napoleon.

**An imaginative rendering entitled "N. Bonaparte, First Consul of the French Republic, Presenting PEACE to the four Quarters of the WORLD."**

Italian campaign. Under his orders, the bronze horses of St. Mark's Cathedral in Venice had been carried off to Paris, along with the *Venus of Medici*, Raphael's *Transfiguration*, and many other famous works. Now, as First Consul, Napoleon commissioned new streets, triumphal arches, fountains and lovely buildings. Paris was to be a glowing center of culture.

On the foreign front, Napoleon brought peace to France and the rest of Europe for a time. With a minimum of fighting, he concluded treaty after treaty that left France the major power on the Continent.

By winning the Battle of Marengo in 1800, Napoleon had broken Austria's hold in northern Italy. Austria was forced to sign the Treaty of Lunéville in 1801. He settled France's differences with Naples and the United States by treaty. He persuaded Tsar Paul I of Russia to leave the anti-French coalition and work with him against Britain. Finally, worn down by the long years of fighting, Britain signed the Treaty of Amiens in 1802. The terms were extremely favorable to France.

By 1802 the effects of Napoleon's leadership were evident everywhere in France. The widespread crime of the post-revolutionary period had ended. Roads, public buildings, and parks had been rebuilt. The schools were better and were open to more people. The study of science and technology was encouraged.

Napoleon made sure that the land given to the peasants during the revolution was legally theirs to keep. His Civil Code guaranteed personal liberty, freedom of conscience, and equality before the law. He portrayed himself not only as the guardian of the French Revolution but as the man who made its ideals a reality.

"We have finished with the romance of the revolution, we must now begin its history," he declared. "We must see what was real and politically possible in its principles, instead of grasping at their speculative and hypothetical side."

Napoleon was just 30 years old when he became First Consul. By the time he signed the Treaty of

An enthusiastic crowd cheers Napoleon as he drives through the streets of Paris. Though a hero to the common people of France, he had countless enemies among the aristocracy. In December 1800 a cart filled with explosives blew up only minutes after his carriage passed by it on the way to the opera, killing 20 people, wounding 53.

Amiens in 1802, he was at the height of his popularity. He had saved France and the revolution from their enemies, and he could do no wrong. But the seeds of his future despotism were already growing.

In December 1800 a wagon filled with explosives had blown up as Napoleon's carriage passed by on the way to the opera. He was furious. He blamed the assassination attempt on left-wing radicals, purged the Council of State, and had many suspects executed. From then on, he clamped down on all persons and institutions that dared to oppose him.

He closed down 64 of the nation's 73 newspapers and censored the theater. He had his librarian prepare reports on every book, journal, placard, and announcement that appeared in France. He demanded summaries of what went on in every club, society, and educational institution. Private letters were opened, people were imprisoned without trial, and leading intellectuals were removed from the parliament. But his military successes and public projects kept the majority of the French people happy. After the Treaty of Amiens, they voted Napoleon First Consul for life.

Napoleon's great power and prestige did not prevent him from keeping an eye on the smallest details, especially where the army was concerned.

A woodcut of the execution of the duke of Enghien, March 21, 1804. Wrongfully implicated in a plot to assassinate Napoleon, the duke was kidnapped from his home in Germany and summarily shot by French soldiers.

*Napoleon as First Consul*, a portrait by Jean Auguste Dominique Ingres (1780–1867). A student of David's, Ingres was noted for the sensuality he injected into his paintings.

Once, one of his officers presented him with an artillery report dealing with thousands of guns in a large coastal area. "Your report is accurate," Napoleon said, "but you have forgotten two of the four guns in Ostend. They are on the high road behind the town."

Another time, reviewing his troops, he noticed that now and then they would raise their hands to their necks. He asked them why they were fidgeting, but no one spoke. Rather than let the matter rest, Napoleon kept at them. He told them not to be afraid of complaining to him. Finally they admitted that the collars on their new uniforms were scratchy and tight. Napoleon immediately had new uniforms made for his men.

Early in 1804 Napoleon's police uncovered another plot against his life. The conspirators were backed by the British and led by Georges Cadoudal, a royalist *émigré*. Napoleon had Cadoudal and his associates arrested, tried, and executed or exiled. He also sent his police across the border into neutral German territory to kidnap the duke of Enghien.

The duke was a member of the French royal family, the Bourbons. Although he was working to overthrow Napoleon and bring back the monarchy, he had nothing to do with the Cadoudal conspiracy. Nevertheless, he was given a hasty trial before a military court and shot on Napoleon's orders. Napoleon probably knew that the duke was innocent in this particular case but had him executed anyway, to terrorize his opponents.

Napoleon was quick to take advantage of the Cadoudal plot. He now said that it was not enough to be First Consul for life. Plots were everywhere, and he might be assassinated at any time. The only way to keep all his work from being destroyed was to make his position a hereditary one. Then, even if he was killed, a child of his or a member of his family could continue his great design for France.

In May 1804 the French parliament proclaimed Napoleon emperor of France and made the title hereditary. Once again the French people were asked to approve the decision in a plebiscite; once again they voted overwhelmingly for their hero, now Emperor Napoleon I.

Once Napoleon decided to be Emperor, his imagination took flight. He saw himself as a new Alexander the Great or Julius Caesar or Charlemagne. Charlemagne was a great French king and conqueror who had tried to help his people by encouraging education and trade. In 800 A.D., a thousand years before Napoleon, Pope Leo III had crowned him Emperor of the West.

Napoleon knew that Charlemagne had laid the foundations of the Holy Roman Empire and was a legendary figure in France. He therefore chose to revive the symbols of Charlemagne's reign. He carried Charlemagne's sword and even set up court briefly at Charlemagne's capital, Aix-la-Chapelle. By wrapping himself in Charlemagne's mantle, Napoleon was sending a powerful message to the other rulers of Europe.

Charlemagne and all the emperors after him had been crowned by the pope in Rome. But Napoleon was determined to bring the pope to Paris for his coronation. Without the pope, the ceremony would

> *I could marry [the Virgin Mary] without shocking the Parisians.*
> —NAPOLEON BONAPARTE

On December 2, 1804, Napoleon anointed himself emperor of France while a rather gloomy Pope Pius VII looked on. David later did a charcoal sketch of this historic event.

David's painting of the coronation of Napoleon and Josephine in Notre Dame Cathedral. After coaxing the pope all the way from Rome for the occasion, Napoleon performed all the honors without any papal assistance, placing the crown on his wife Josephine's head just as he had done for himself.

*Napoleon is the posthumous brother of Dante and of Michelangelo; in view of the definite contours of his vision, the intensity, the coherence, and inner consistency of his dream, the depth of his meditations, the superhuman greatness of his conception, he is their equal: his genius has the same size and the same structure; he is one of the three sovereign spirits of the Italian Renaissance.*

—HIPPOLYTE TAINE
French philosopher/critic

be incomplete. The pope in question was Pius VII, the same one who had signed the Concordat of 1801.

Napoleon hinted that he would strengthen Catholicism in France in exchange for the pope's cooperation. It was a rather vague offer, but the feeble head of the Catholic church agreed to cross the Alps. The pope's presence made it seem that the coronation had the blessing of God himself.

Napoleon saw to it that no expense was spared. Armies of seamstresses and interior decorators went to work to prepare for the great event. Then the pope discovered that Napoleon and Josephine had only been married in a civil ceremony. He insisted that they have a religious wedding before they were crowned emperor and empress of France.

The coronation took place in the cathedral of Notre Dame on December 2, 1804. Napoleon and

Josephine set out for Notre Dame in a magnificent carriage. They were two hours late and kept the pope waiting in the freezing cathedral. Dressed in velvet, lace, and silk embroidered with gold and silver, they finally appeared.

The ceremony began. When the moment came for the pope to place the crown on Napoleon's head, Napoleon snatched it from the shivering pontiff's hands. Turning his back on the pope, he placed the crown on his own head. Napoleon had crowned himself!

Napoleon then crowned Josephine and took his seat upon the throne. Turning to his brother Joseph, he said in a low voice, "If only our father could see us!"

His mother, Letizia, now a feisty lady of 54, had a different reaction: "So long as it lasts . . . ."

> *It may be that once his soul had sunk so low as to see no more greatness except in despotism, he became incapable of managing without perpetual war: for what would a despot be without perpetual war?*
> —Mme. DE STAËL
> French writer

Napoleon's mother, Letizia, (1750–1836), the rock of the Bonaparte family, kept a level head amidst all the pomp of empire, and prayed that it would last.

# 6

# Birth of an Empire

$N$apoleon's mind was never still. Once he became emperor, a position in which he might have relaxed, he kept right on going.

His day started at about 7:00 A.M. He began by reading letters, reports, and dispatches—even those not addressed to him. He always had a secretary by his side, and he dictated streams of directives and other correspondence. These were immediately sent to the proper department.

The rest of his day was filled with meetings, receptions, and tours of inspection. During all this activity, he never stopped dictating memos and instructions. He continued to attend meetings of the Council of State, some of which lasted far into the night. When his tired ministers began falling asleep, he would wake them up and laughingly tell them to get back to work and earn the money France was paying them.

He could go for a long time without sleep, and worked his way through three or four tired secretaries a day. He did not like to take time out for meals and often made Josephine and his court wait for hours. One day 23 chickens were cooked one after the other so there would always be a chicken cooked just to the emperor's taste, no matter when he chose to eat it.

The peace that followed the Treaty of Amiens

Napoleon I, emperor of the French Republic, as portrayed by François Gérard (1770–1837). Napoleon was never troubled by the seeming contradiction between "Emperor" and "Republic." He continued to portray himself as the savior of the Revolution even while creating a new aristocracy and restoring many of the rituals of monarchy.

The French surrender the Mediterranean island of Malta to the British in September 1800. Malta, the first conquest of Napoleon's Egyptian campaign, was retaken by the British after a two-year siege. Britain's refusal to return the island to the Maltese under the terms of the 1802 Treaty of Amiens triggered the renewal of hostilities between France and Britain in 1803.

Napoleon parceled out his newly enlarged empire among his relatives. He made his brother Joseph (above) king of Naples and promoted him to king of Spain in 1808.

lasted about a year and a half. The British had never really trusted Napoleon. When he continued to meddle in the affairs of Italy, Germany, and other parts of Europe, they became even more suspicious. In May 1803 they broke the Treaty of Amiens. France was once again at war with her old enemy.

Napoleon made plans to launch an invasion against Britain. He built up the French navy and massed his troops at Boulogne, on the English Channel. He also put his engineers to work on a variety of clever but impractical schemes, such as digging a tunnel under the Channel or landing the invasion forces by balloon.

Napoleon was not a naval officer. He understood artillery, sieges, and swift movements over land, but he did not understand wind, waves, fog, and currents. Once, during a fierce storm, he ordered one of his admirals to hold a scheduled review of the fleet. The admiral refused. Napoleon dismissed him, and the review proceeded. As a result, many ships were damaged or sunk, and 200 men drowned.

In October 1805 Admiral Nelson trapped the French navy at Cape Trafalgar, off the coast of Spain. As he had done before at Aboukir Bay during Napoleon's Egyptian expedition, he crushed the French. Though he lost his life in the Battle of Trafalgar, Nelson won a decisive victory for Britain and shattered Napoleon's dreams of conquest by sea.

Meanwhile, Napoleon's actions had antagonized other nations besides Britain. When the duke of Enghien was executed in 1804, all the monarchs of Europe were outraged, especially Tsar Alexander I of Russia. Shortly thereafter, when Napoleon crowned himself emperor of France in the tradition of Charlemagne, he insulted Emperor Francis II of Austria. Francis held the title of Holy Roman emperor and considered himself the legitimate heir of Charlemagne. In 1805, when Napoleon took over Genoa and proclaimed himself king of Italy as well, Francis was even angrier. Now it was not just a matter of titles and wounded pride—Austria's territory in Italy was at stake.

Thus, even as Napoleon was planning to attack Britain, he was making enemies of the very countries Britain wanted as allies. In the summer of 1805, Britain joined with Russia, Austria, Sweden, and Naples to form the Third Coalition.

Napoleon was ready for them. In July he ordered his army—an imposing force of some 200,000 men, now called the Grand Army—away from the English Channel and into Germany. There, the week before the naval defeat at Trafalgar, he met the Austrians at Ulm and beat them easily. In November he marched into Vienna, and on December 2, 1805, he wiped out the combined Russian and Austrian armies at Austerlitz. It was one of the greatest victories of his career.

After Austerlitz, Tsar Alexander's troops retreated, but Russia remained at war with France. Austria

When war broke out between Britain and France in 1803, Napoleon reactivated the various invasion plans that he and his staff had been considering since 1798. In addition to such sensible steps as building up his navy, he impractically entertained notions of landing troops by balloon and tunneling beneath the English Channel.

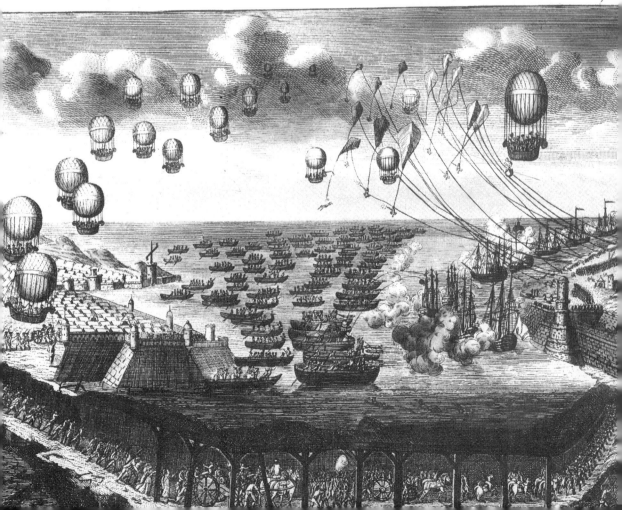

signed the Treaty of Pressburg, giving up its Italian possessions and recognizing Napoleon as king of Italy. Austria also agreed to the creation of several German states allied with France. In 1806 Napoleon united these states with several others in western Germany to form the Confederation of the Rhine. That same year, Francis II gave up his title as Holy Roman emperor.

All this time, Prussia had remained neutral. Now, worried by the defeat of Austria, the Prussians declared war on France. On October 14, 1806, Napoleon's forces met them in battle at Jena and Auerstädt. Although the Prussians fought hard, they could not change their tactics fast enough to

**After beating the Austrians at Ulm in October 1805, Napoleon reviewed the defeated troops and praised their courage. He took 30,000 prisoners and packed them off to France with the words: "On seeing the spirit which animates my people, you will rally round my standard."**

keep up with Napoleon's shifting plan of battle. In these two bitter engagements Napoleon and his generals smashed the Prussian army, taking 25,000 prisoners.

Napoleon's victory at Jena had special meaning for him. Under Frederick the Great, a leader Napoleon admired, Prussia had once been the greatest military power in Europe. Now, in a single day, Napoleon had brought Prussia to its knees. The legend of his military genius was growing by leaps and bounds.

With the exception of Britain and Russia, Napoleon was now master of most of Europe. Since he had lost his fleet at Trafalgar, and could no longer hope to defeat Britain at sea, he came up with another plan of attack—the Continental System. Under this system, Napoleon ordered the countries of Europe to stop trading with Britain. He hoped to ruin British industry and force his enemy into bankruptcy. But the system was difficult to enforce and did not work very well. One of its main results was an active smuggling trade.

While waging economic warfare against Britain,

**Napoleon meets with Francis II of Austria after the Battle of Austerlitz, on December 2, 1805. Facing a combined Austro-Russian force, Napoleon won what is considered the most brilliant victory of his career at Austerlitz. There is a famous description of the battle in *War and Peace*, a novel by Russian author Leo Tolstoy (1828–1910).**

Napoleon at the Battle of Jena, as portrayed by Carle Vernat (1758–1835). Continuing his extraordinary string of victories, Napoleon decisively defeated the once-mighty Prussian army at Jena in October 1806.

Napoleon marched into Poland to meet the Russians. Unfortunately, much of Poland was a wilderness, and there was no way for the army to feed itself off the land. Napoleon had to set up long and vulnerable supply lines. To make matters worse, winter was approaching.

It was during his stay in Poland that Napoleon had a passionate love affair with an 18-year-old Polish girl named Maria Walewska. Since the 1770s Poland had been divided between Austria, Prussia, and Russia. Many Poles looked to Napoleon to free their country and restore its independence. Maria was one of them.

The wife of an aging Polish count, she had disguised herself as a peasant girl and stopped Napoleon's carriage to beg for peace and liberty for Poland. She then disappeared into the crowd, but not before Napoleon had fallen hopelessly in love. Demanding that his officers locate her, Napoleon went to Warsaw, the Polish capital. When Maria was finally found, Napoleon sent her a special invitation to attend a ball and enclosed a bouquet of flowers made of diamonds. Maria flatly refused. She was a very virtuous girl.

It seemed that all of Poland tried to change her mind. Everyone believed that she alone could persuade Napoleon to restore Poland to its original boundaries and former glory. Even her friends felt that it was her patriotic duty to sacrifice her own feelings and become Napoleon's mistress. Finally, unable to resist such pressure, she gave in.

But then Maria actually fell in love with him. She left her husband and made the winter of 1806–07 a very romantic one for Napoleon, if not for his freezing soldiers.

On February 8, 1807, Napoleon's army, now shrunk to about 55,000 men, met a Russian force of 80,000 at Eylau. It was snowing, and the battleground was a sea of mud. Napoleon was disorga-

*For Poland, God created a fifth element: mud.*
—NAPOLEON BONAPARTE speaking in 1807, shortly after the Battle of Eylau

**Napoleon's victory at Austerlitz placed him firmly in control of most of Continental Europe, and left Britain his only real rival as a world power. This caricature by James Gillray shows Napoleon and British Prime Minister William Pitt (1759–1806) dividing up the world.**

The Polish patriot Maria Walewska (1789–1817) became Napoleon's mistress for her country's sake but then fell in love with him. In 1810 she bore him a son, Count Alexandre Walewski (1810–1868), who fought for Polish independence and later served as a French diplomat during the reign of his cousin Napoleon III (1808–1873).

*The life of Europe was centered in one man; all were trying to fill their lungs with the air he breathed. Every year France presented that man with three hundred thousand of her youth; it was the tax paid to Caesar, and, without that troop behind him, he could not follow his fortune.*

—ALFRED DE MUSSET

nized and at his worst as a commander. At the last minute, two fresh divisions arrived, saving the French army from collapse. The battle ended in stalemate, with heavy casualties on both sides. "Never have I seen so many dead collected in such a small space," one French general later wrote. "Whole divisions, Russian and French, had been hacked to pieces where they stood."

When news of the bloodshed and near defeat reached France, the people grew troubled. Napoleon sent urgent messages to his foreign minister, Talleyrand, demanding supplies and more men. The French military schools sent their students, and various countries controlled by France were also forced to send troops. In May 1807, with his battered Grand Army and these raw new recruits, Napoleon set off after the Russians once more.

On June 14, 1807—an important date to the superstitious emperor, since it was the seventh anniversary of his victory at Marengo—Napoleon defeated the Russians at Friedland. Tsar Alexander had the manpower and resources to continue the war, but he was tired of fighting. He agreed to negotiate.

The Russian tsar and the French emperor met on a raft moored in the middle of the Niemen River. With much display and ceremony, the two men conferred. Soon it appeared that a real friendship was blossoming. They were joined by Frederick William of Prussia, whom they both considered stuffy and boring. They avoided his company as much as possible and spent long hours deep in conversation. The young tsar was awed by the great Napoleon, who repaid the admiration by saying, "Were Alexander a woman, I think I should fall madly in love with him!"

In February 1807 the Russians regrouped and made a stand against Napoleon at Eylau, nearly defeating him in a long, bloody battle.

Early in July 1807 the three rulers signed the Treaty of Tilsit. Frederick William lost heavily on the deal. Prussia was forced to cede all its territory west of the Elbe River, lost half its population, and was also coerced into participating in the Continental System. Russia lost only a few possessions on the Mediterranean and agreed to recognize the Grand Duchy of Warsaw, a state created by Napoleon out of the Prussian part of Poland. Alexander also agreed to act as mediator in the war between France and Britain, and to ally himself with France if negotiations failed. Twenty days later Napoleon was back in Paris.

His empire was now vast. To keep it under control, he resorted to the age-old method of dividing it among relatives. He made his brother Joseph king of Naples, which had been a member of the

**Admiral Horatio Nelson, Napoleon's great maritime adversary. In 1798 he had destroyed the French fleet in the Battle of the Nile; in October 1805 he did it again, at the Battle of Trafalgar, though the victory cost him his life.**

Napoleon welcomes Tsar Alexander I (1777–1825) to his raft on the Niemen River near Tilsit in 1807. After Napoleon defeated the Russians at Friedland, the tsar decided to negotiate. The floating peace talks produced the Treaty of Tilsit, which consolidated Napoleon's immense power.

defeated Third Coalition. His brother Louis married Josephine's daughter Hortense, and they became king and queen of the Netherlands. His brother Jérôme, became king of Westphalia, a former Prussian territory. Jérôme married Catherine, daughter of the king of Württemberg, another German ally of France.

General Murat, who had married Napoleon's sister Caroline, was made grand duke of Berg, in

Napoleon's sister Caroline (1782–1839), at first only a grand duchess, became a queen when Napoleon made her husband, Joachim Murat, king of Naples.

Germany, and later succeeded Joseph Bonaparte as king of Naples. Napoleon's two other sisters held Italian titles: Elisa was grand duchess of Tuscany, and Pauline, princess of Guastalla. Eugène de Beauharnais, Josephine's son, served ably as viceroy of Italy. Count Bernadotte, Joseph's brother-in-law, became prince of Ponte Corvo in 1806 and heir to the Swedish throne in 1809. Bernadotte was the man who had married Désirée Clary shortly after Napoleon had ceased to pay attention to her.

It was all very well to keep the empire in the family, but Napoleon still did not have a child of his own. Though his title was hereditary, there was no direct heir to take his place if he should die. Family squabbles had already begun to sim-

78

mer, making him anxious about the fate of his domains.

At the same time, Napoleon's relations with his foreign minister, Talleyrand, were growing strained. Talleyrand was a wily old nobleman who had not only survived the upheavals of revolutionary France but profited from them. He had attached himself to Napoleon very early, when he saw that the young general was destined for greatness.

Now he began to believe that Napoleon's fame and power had gone to his head. He thought that international stability required a balance among all the major powers of Europe, and he feared Napoleon's designs on the entire Continent. But the more he advised caution, the more the emperor ignored him.

Carefully, and with utmost skill, Talleyrand began plotting behind Napoleon's back. He gradually broke Tsar Alexander's infatuation with Napoleon and worked secretly to strengthen Austria. Napoleon's restless ambition would probably have caused his downfall eventually, without any outside help. But Talleyrand spotted the first signs of weakness in his emperor and exploited them ruthlessly.

> *If Napoleon is welcomed by North America, she will be attacked by all Europe.*
> —SIMÓN BOLÍVAR
> South American revolutionary

**Charles Maurice de Talleyrand, Napoleon's foreign minister. A member of the high aristocracy, he somehow weathered the mighty tempests of the Revolution, aided Napoleon in his rise from general to emperor, and helped to engineer his eventual downfall when he began to fear Napoleon's ambition.**

NAPOLEON

# 7

# The Empire Unravels

Napoleon wanted a divorce. In all their years of marriage, Josephine had borne him no children. Because she already had two children by her first husband, Napoleon had always thought the problem was his.

Shortly after his victories at Austerlitz and Jena, Napoleon learned that he was a father. The previous spring, he had had a brief affair with a young woman named Eleonore Revel, who gave birth to a baby boy. The news arrived just as he was falling in love with Maria Walewska. Soon Maria was also pregnant.

Convinced that he could have children, Napoleon made up his mind to get rid of Josephine. It took him two years to complete the arrangements. He and Josephine had had a stormy relationship, and each had been unfaithful to the other. Still, she was one of the best friends he had. He was used to her, and he was always very good to those who had helped him in his youth. Besides, Napoleon truly loved Josephine. It was a hard decision for him to make, but his self-centered need to establish a dynasty finally won.

This time, Napoleon wanted to marry into one of the ruling families of Europe. In 1808 he met with Tsar Alexander at Erfurt, hoping to sign a treaty of

*His life was the stride of a demigod from battle to battle and from victory to victory. . . . It could be said that he was in a permanent state of enlightenment, which is why his fate was more brilliant than the world has ever seen or is likely to see after him.*
—GOETHE
German writer

**When Napoleon told his wife that he wanted a divorce because she had given him no heir to the throne, she threw an imperial tantrum, fainted, and had to be carried to her bedchamber.**

An idealized rendering of Napoleon in 1812 by Louis Girodet (1767–1824), a painter with a penchant for romanticism who devoted much of his career to the glorification of his beloved emperor.

alliance against Austria. He also asked for the hand of Alexander's sister, the Grand Duchess Anna. Under the influence of Talleyrand, the tsar turned down both proposals. Napoleon would have to look elsewhere for what he called "a womb"—a woman to give him a child.

Meanwhile, at the height of his power, he began to overreach himself. Late in 1807 he decided to make war on Portugal, which had refused to participate in the Continental System. The Spanish king, Charles IV, agreed to let Napoleon march his army through Spain to launch the attack against the Portuguese.

King Charles was very unpopular among his own people. In 1808 they rose against him in favor of his son, Ferdinand VII. Napoleon was quick to take advantage of the situation. He kept sending more and more troops into Spain, on the excuse that they were reinforcements for his army in Portugal.

Charles IV of Spain (at right; 1748–1819), and his son Ferdinand VII (at center; 1784–1833) with the French emperor at Talleyrand's chateau in 1808. In one of the most underhanded moves of his entire career, Napoleon lured them both to France and placed them under house arrest, forcing them to abdicate in favor of his brother Joseph.

Then he lured Charles and Ferdinand to France. After forcing both of them into giving up their claim to the Spanish throne, he locked them up in Talleyrand's villa and proclaimed his brother Joseph king of Spain.

Just as Napoleon was congratulating himself on adding another kingdom to his collection, the Spanish revolted. They did not like Charles, but they loved Ferdinand, and they hated the French. All over the countryside the people rose up against the invaders.

Spain was too big, too rugged, too barren, and too poor to support the French troops. Supply lines were constantly collapsing. The army could not fight because there were never any real battles. Spaniards of all ages attacked from hills and caves, then disappeared into hiding. It was guerrilla warfare, and it was eating away at the morale of the French soldiers.

Soon Britain came to the aid of Portugal, where the people were also in revolt. The French suffered a major defeat in August 1808. They were driven out of Portugal and retreated to Spain, pursued by the British.

*A man of no convictions, no habits, no traditions, no name, not even a Frenchman, by the strangest freaks of chance, as it seems, rises above the seething parties of France, and without attaching himself to any one of them, advances to a prominent position.*
—LEO TOLSTOY
Russian writer

Having divorced his wife, Napoleon married Marie Louise (1791–1847), daughter of Emperor Francis II of Austria, on April 2, 1810. Marie, who proved to be an opportunistic empress, deserted Napoleon in 1814 during his darkest hour and ran home to her parents.

*I want to contemplate, under the weight of that admirable machine, society flattened, stifled, and increasingly sterile, intellectual activity slowing down, human mind languishing, souls shrinking, great men ceasing to appear, and a limitless, flat horizon against which nothing can be seen, no matter in which direction one's eyes may turn, save the colossal figure [of Napoleon] himself.*
— ALEXIS DE TOCQUEVILLE
19th-century French historian

Instead of cutting his losses, Napoleon sent most of his Grand Army to Spain. Late in 1808 he went to Spain himself to take personal command of his men. The conflict—known as the Peninsular War, because Spain and Portugal together occupy a land mass called the Iberian Peninsula—raged back and forth across the two countries, with no clear victory on either side.

Knowing that it would be difficult for France to fight on two fronts, Austria's Archduke Charles crossed the border into Bavaria in April 1809 and took Napoleon by surprise. Suddenly he was at war with Austria for the fourth time, and his best troops were still in Spain. Nevertheless, he managed to beat the Austrians back and chase them all the way to Vienna.

At the two-day battle of Aspern, Napoleon's army took heavy losses. In July 1809 he outmaneuvered the Austrians at Wagram. It was a costly, bloody battle for both sides, but Napoleon emerged triumphant. In October the Austrians signed the Treaty of Schönbrunn.

Shortly afterwards, Emperor Francis of Austria agreed to a marriage between Napoleon and his 18-year-old daughter, Archduchess Marie Louise. Why were Austria and France, so recently at war, ready to walk down the aisle together? Because Francis thought the marriage would soften Napoleon's attitude to Austria, and Napoleon thought it would strengthen his hold on Francis. As an added attraction, Napoleon found out that Marie Louise's mother had had 13 children! He quickly divorced Josephine, in December 1809.

Though not the prettiest or wittiest of girls, this new bride-to-be excited Napoleon tremendously. Impressed by the fact that she was a real princess, he went out of his way to treat her royally. He had her personal rooms redecorated and smothered her with costly gifts. He got himself a new tailor and a new

*Napoleon at Wagram*, **a painting by Vernet. In April 1809 the Austrians took advantage of Napoleon's preoccupation with the Spanish war and attacked him in the east. After a defeat at Aspern, he beat them back at Wagram, and by October they were forced to sue for peace.**

On March 20, 1811, Empress Marie Louise presented Napoleon with a son and heir: François - Charles - Joseph (d.1832), king of Rome, who showed signs of true imperial fortitude by sitting for this portrait at 14 months of age.

shoemaker so he would look more elegant. He even learned the latest dance—the waltz.

As for poor Marie Louise, she was horrified by her future husband. To her, Napoleon was the monster who kept beating her father's armies and snatching his lands. He was hated and feared by the royalty of Europe, most of whom were her relatives. He was over 40 years old, and she was a mere child. As if all that were not enough, he was shorter than she was!

The wedding took place in the spring of 1810. Napoleon turned on the charm for his new empress, who overcame her initial horror and began to grow fond of him. Marie Louise was soon pregnant with Napoleon's much-wanted heir. On March 20, 1811, she gave birth to a boy—François-Charles-Joseph, king of Rome.

It was fortunate that Napoleon was happy with his new family, because his old one was causing him a lot of trouble. First, there was his brother Lucien, who had defended him in the Council of Five Hundred back in 1799. After Napoleon became First Consul, Lucien opposed his dictatorial policies. He eventually settled in Italy and was made prince of Canino by Pope Pius. By 1810, relations between Napoleon and Pius were more strained than they had ever been before  Napoleon had taken over Rome and the Papal States. When the pope then excommunicated Napoleon, the French emperor had Pius arrested. Lucien fled and was captured by the British.

Then there were brothers Louis, Joseph, and Jérôme. Louis abandoned the throne of the Netherlands rather than obey Napoleon's order to blockade British trade goods. Joseph, king of Spain, wanted to put an end to the divisions that were plaguing his country and become a true leader of the Spanish people. Though Napoleon forced him to continue the Peninsular War, his heart was not in it. The youngest brother, King Jérôme of Westphalia, was more interested in affairs of the heart than affairs of state.

Napoleon's sisters were not much help either. Princess Pauline was a flighty, vain woman who got into one scandal after another. Grand Duchess Elisa did pay some attention to governing Tuscany but took more interest in gaining publicity. Queen Caroline of Naples was the worst. She had hoped that her son might succeed Napoleon. Once he had his own child, there was no chance of that, so she and her husband began actively plotting against the man who had given them their thrones.

And then there was Bernadotte, Napoleon's general, who had become crown prince of Sweden with Napoleon's support. By 1810 the aging king of Sweden was no longer able to govern effectively, and Bernadotte held the real power. Like Louis and Joseph, he too took his new job seriously. From now on, his first loyalty was to Sweden, not Napoleon.

To outward appearances, Napoleon's empire was at its greatest in 1810. But the discontent within his family was a sign of deeper troubles. The war in Spain was costing money and lives, and there was no end in sight. Napoleon's ties with Russia had grown weaker since the Treaty of Tilsit. He had many enemies, in France and abroad, who might strike at the first sign of weakness. His blockade of England was becoming increasingly difficult

*Napoleon, then, is a nineteenth-century tyrant. Who says tyrant says superior mind; and it is inconceivable that a superior mind can fail to absorb the common-sense ideas that are in the air. It is very curious to follow in Napoleon's soul the struggle between the genius of tyranny and the deep rationality that made a great man of him.*
—STENDHAL
19th-century French writer

**Napoleon's empire was at its height in 1812. He had essentially consolidated his power by 1810, and over the next few years found himself confronted with increased tensions in various corners of his many and far-flung dominions.**

to enforce. Worse, it was not really hurting England, but it *was* hurting Napoleon. It made him look like a tyrant to the rest of Europe.

In 1811, because of the pressing economic needs of his country, Tsar Alexander decided to defy the Continental System. He opened his ports to British shipping, thus resuming trade relations with France's greatest enemy. In December of that year, Napoleon started planning the invasion of Russia. It was to be the biggest military venture in history up to that time.

At this point in his career, Napoleon's image had become a little tarnished. No longer the lean and hard military commander of the old days, he managed nevertheless to inspire his troops, exercising all the skills of an actor. He assembled a huge army

When Napoleon marched into Russia with his Grand Army of half a million men, the enemy troops retreated before him, destroying livestock, crops, and equipment as they went. Unable to replenish their supplies, Napoleon's soldiers suffered greatly from hunger, and foraging parties often came under attack from armed and irate peasants.

of half a million men, including contingents from Prussia, the Confederation of the Rhine, and all the other states under his control. Within six months, he was ready.

On June 24, 1812, with this grandest Grand Army of all, Napoleon crossed the Niemen River and entered Russia. It was the same river upon which he and Tsar Alexander had met aboard a raft and conversed so intimately five years before.

Napoleon had seriously underestimated the difficulty of moving such an enormous force across the vast territory of Russia. His men soon ate the food they had brought with them and wandered off in search of supplies. They found little, and many were killed or captured by Cossacks, the fierce peasant cavalry of the Ukraine.

The summer heat was terrible. The horses ate green hay and corn from the fields, and 10,000 of them died in those first weeks. With the cavalry weakened, the transport of artillery and supplies was almost impossible. Even worse, the Russian army was retreating ahead of Napoleon, filling in wells and burning fields and towns as they went. This scorched-earth policy made the French advance terribly difficult.

If Napoleon had been able to meet the Russians early in the campaign, he would probably have defeated them. His forces greatly outnumbered theirs. But the Russians refused him the favor. The tsar had learned a lesson from British tactics in Spain: avoid pitched battles. More and more dying men, dead horses, and abandoned wagons littered the road the French army traveled as it chased the foe deeper and deeper into Russia. After more than two months, there still had not been a single battle.

On September 7, 1812, Napoleon finally caught up with the Russians at Borodino, 70 miles west of Moscow, some 400 miles into Russia. By now, death, desertion, illness, and Cossack ambushes had reduced his army to little more than half its original strength. To make things worse, Napoleon had a bad cold and a bladder infection. As the day wore on, he took less and less interest in the battle and

**By 1812 Napoleon was showing signs of wear and tear, but his appetite for conquest remained keen as he planned the invasion of Russia.**

On September 14, 1812, Napoleon entered Moscow, expecting that his capture of the city would force concessions from Tsar Alexander I. Instead Moscow was totally empty, and shortly after Napoleon's arrival it burned to the ground in a huge conflagration.

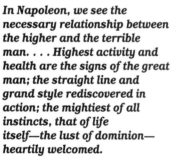

*In Napoleon, we see the necessary relationship between the higher and the terrible man. . . . Highest activity and health are the signs of the great man; the straight line and grand style rediscovered in action; the mightiest of all instincts, that of life itself—the lust of dominion— heartily welcomed.*

—FRIEDRICH NIETZSCHE
19th-century German
philosopher

left his generals to conduct the fighting as they saw fit. The French did manage to force a Russian retreat, but only at great cost to themselves. Napoleon lost between 30,000 and 40,000 men, and the Russian army had merely fallen back. It had not conceded. Still, the road to Moscow lay open at last.

At noon on September 14, the Grand Army—now down to 100,000 men—marched through the gates of the ancient capital of the tsars. Napoleon expected to be handed the keys of the city and received as a conqueror. Then, with Moscow held hostage, he would force Alexander to negotiate.

But the golden spires and domes of the Kremlin, the city's mighty fortress, looked down on a ghost town. There was hardly a Muscovite to be seen. The French troops moved through the deserted streets into the empty houses, but no sooner had they settled in than mysterious fires began to break out everywhere. Soon Napoleon was the unchallenged master of a city reduced to little more than ashes.

The tsar would not negotiate. He had his own plan. Russia itself would defeat Napoleon's army. He would delay Napoleon in Moscow until the frigid Russian winter could finish off the hated invader. Napoleon waited and waited for word from Alexander. None came. On October 18 it began to snow lightly. The next day, he finally began his retreat.

He tried the Kaluga road, where there was food and water. But on October 23, at the town of Maloyaroslavetz, the Russian army forced him back to the road he had used on the way in—the shattered Smolensk road.

At the end of October the cold set in with a

Napoleon at the Battle of Borodino, his first engagement with the Russians after more than two months on the march. After savage fighting and tremendous casualties on both sides, the Russians retreated, and Napoleon pressed on to Moscow.

The Grand Army in retreat, as depicted by a German eyewitness. Napoleon was forced to march out of Russia by the same route he had used while entering it. Again, supplies for his troops were woefully lacking, and by now the bitter Russian winter had set in.

> The Empire is an old serving woman who is used to being raped by everyone.
> —NAPOLEON BONAPARTE
> speaking with reference to the German Empire

vengeance. The temperature fell to 20 degrees below zero. Horses slipped on the ice, broke their legs, and had to be shot. Soldiers dropped dead from starvation and cold. All the stolen treasures of Moscow—gold, silver, paintings, jewels, candelabra, icons, ornate crosses littered the roadside, where they kept grotesque company with the corpses and abandoned artillery.

André Castelot, in his book *Napoleon*, describes the horror of the retreat from Moscow: "Ravens froze in midflight and fell to the ground. Exhaled breath froze when it came in contact with the air, making a sharp little popping sound. . . . Many of the survivors were walking barefoot using pieces of wood as canes, but their feet were frozen so hard that the sound they made on the road was like that of wooden clogs."

On November 26, 1812, the Grand Army—now down to 26,000 troops, along with 40,000 army followers including women and children—reached the freezing Beresina River. The bridges had been destroyed, and the crossing took three days. Russian troops and Cossacks kept up a constant attack. Thousands of French troops were killed, drowned, or left behind to be massacred.

Everything seemed to be going wrong for the once invincible emperor. On one occasion, he himself was almost captured by Cossacks, and the Russian troops had been instructed to pay special attention to captured French soldiers "of small stature." Napoleon vowed that he would never be taken prisoner and began to wear a dose of poison around his neck in a silk pouch.

Meanwhile, news of the catastrophe in Russia had reached France and the rest of Europe. Everywhere, Napoleon's enemies rejoiced and began to plot his downfall. Talleyrand was busier than ever working to restore the old French monarchy. In Paris, a certain General Malet announced that Napoleon had been killed on the battlefield, and almost succeeded in taking over the government. When Napoleon learned of the attempted coup, he deserted what was left of his army and rushed back to Paris.

It had taken Napoleon 16 years to subdue the whole of Europe and rise to the heights of power. By the time another 16 months, had elapsed, everything he had accomplished would lie in ruins at his feet.

The fording of the Beresina River, November 26, 1812. Under heavy attack by the Russians, more than 20,000 Frenchmen perished in the crossing, but Napoleon's army—at least what was left of it—escaped capture.

# 8

# Death of an Empire, Birth of a Legend

The disaster in Russia destroyed the original source of Napoleon's power—his army. Of the half-million men who marched against the tsar, less than 10,000 survived. Any other general might have been utterly ruined by this staggering waste of life. Napoleon only said, "My army took some losses."

Without realizing it, Napoleon had helped to sow the seeds of his own destruction. By pulling together bits and pieces of Italy and Germany, he made them more unified than they had ever been before. He established efficient governments and spread the ideals of the French Revolution. He shook the old monarchies and awakened the slumbering masses of Europe. The very forces that made it possible for Napoleon to dominate the Continent—nationalism, patriotism, hatred of tyranny—were now turned against him.

In Prussia, after popular uprisings against the French, King Frederick William abandoned his alliance with Napoleon and signed a treaty with the tsar. Britain quickly joined them. Bernadotte, once a marshal of Napoleon's empire, brought Sweden into the coalition against his native country. Emperor Francis II of Austria delayed the longest—not

**At the Battle of Lutzen, in May 1813, Napoleon achieved a notable victory with an army that was mainly composed of raw and untried troops. Despite the incredible losses sustained in the Russian campaign, Napoleon had managed to raise another army to defend his crumbling empire.**

**Napoleon in 1814, on the eve of his abdication, as portrayed by Paul Delaroche (1797–1856).**

A German caricature of Napoleon as a nutcracker, with Leipzig as the "tough nut to crack." In the three-day Battle of Leipzig, also known as the Battle of the Nations, Napoleon was defeated by the allied armies of Austria, Russia, and Prussia.

because he was Napoleon's father-in-law, but because he wanted to make sure he chose the winning side. Finally, on August 10, 1813, Austria too declared war.

The spectacle of his enemies gathering for the kill seemed to breathe new life into Napoleon. He became General Bonaparte again, taking command of the situation, working far into the night, issuing orders right and left. By pressuring the Confederation of the Rhine for support and taking men wherever he could find them, he managed to raise another large army, almost 200,000 strong.

Napoleon won some impressive victories against the Russians and Prussians in the spring of 1813. But in June, under the command of Arthur Wellesley (soon to become the duke of Wellington), the British drove the French out of Spain. By October, Wellesley was at the Pyrenees, on the southwestern border of France, ready to invade. At the same time, the armies of the anti-French coalition were on the move in the east, and Napoleon's German allies were beginning to desert him. There were simply too many battles to fight, on too many fronts.

On October 16, 1813, Napoleon took his stand at Leipzig, in eastern Germany. Vastly outnumbered by the combined forces of Austria, Russia, and Prussia, the French army inflicted heavier losses than it sustained. Nevertheless, after three days of fighting, Napoleon was decisively defeated and forced to retreat. This bloody and terrible confrontation—known as the Battle of the Nations—was the beginning of the end for Napoleon.

Throughout 1813, the allies had made several offers of peace on fairly generous terms. Their basic demand was that France return to its borders of 1792. Napoleon refused to settle. He still believed in the force of his genius. He still believed in his empire. He still believed he could rally the French people.

Miraculously, he conjured up another army. His wars had squandered so many lives that he was forced to call up younger and younger men each year. By now his soldiers were practically children. They barely knew one end of the musket from another. Even so, in 1814 he waged an impressive campaign.

Despite his brilliance on the battlefield, Napoleon now faced impossible odds. His troops were hopelessly outnumbered. He could hold his enemies at bay, but he did not have the resources to defeat them utterly. The French people were tired of their emperor and his endless wars, tired of making sacrifices. And Austria, Russia, Prussia, and Britain were united in their determination to bring Napoleon down.

On March 30, 1814, while Napoleon was directing operations east of Paris, the allied armies maneuvered their way past the French forces undetected and entered the city. Napoleon immediately made plans to recapture his capital, but his generals flatly refused. For the first time since the siege of Toulon he was a commander without troops.

In Paris, Talleyrand was doing his best to assure Napoleon's downfall. He persuaded the allies and the temporary French government to offer the throne to Louis XVIII, brother of Louis XVI, the king who was beheaded by the French revolutionaries in 1793. Napoleon tried to hold out, hoping against hope for a miracle, dreaming that an outraged nation would rush to arms in his defense. Finally, on April 6, he was forced to abdicate. Bonaparte was gone; the Bourbons were back.

*After making a mistake or suffering a misfortune, the man of genius always gets back on his feet.*
—NAPOLEON BONAPARTE
while in exile on Elba

**Allied troops enter Paris on March 30, 1814. They were welcomed by the royalists, who thought that the victorious powers would restore the French monarchy.**

Napoleon bids a very emotional farewell to his imperial guard at Fontainebleu before going into exile on the tiny island of Elba.

Filled with despair, he took poison in an attempt to kill himself. But the poison, dating from the disastrous retreat from Russia in 1812, had lost its potency. Napoleon survived, only to be sent into what the allies thought would be permanent exile on the island of Elba. Traveling through France on his way there, he encountered hostile crowds shouting, "Tyrant!" and "Butcher!" For his own safety he had to finish the journey in disguise.

Elba lay off the coast of Italy a few miles from Corsica, his homeland. By the terms of his agreement with the allies, Elba belonged to Napoleon. He took a small guard of several hundred men with him and was allowed to keep his title. The ruler of most of Europe was now the emperor of Elba—all 86 square miles of it.

The French people may have had enough of Napoleon for a while, but that did not mean that they wanted a Bourbon king back on the throne. They did not trust Louis XVIII and all the royalist *émigrés* he brought with him. They considered him a tool of foreign powers and a threat to the gains of the revolution. Realizing this, Napoleon thought he could harness their discontent to his own and reconquer France.

On the clear, starry night of February 26, 1815, Napoleon escaped from Elba with an army of 1,000 men. Some were nervous about the expedition, so Napoleon lied to them. He told them there had already been an uprising in Paris and the people were just waiting for his arrival.

Near Grenoble his old troops, now in the service of the king, tried to stop him. He stood his ground: "If any one of you wishes to kill his general and emperor, let him do it here; here I am." Instead of firing, the men cheered. Once inside Grenoble, he was startled to find that the people had brought him the shattered gates of the city: "They would

**The citizens of Elba present their new emperor with the keys to the island, which was only a few miles away from Corsica, Napoleon's birthplace.**

not give you the keys, so we brought you the door."

When he marched into Lyons, there was cheering in the streets. When he left he had an army of 14,000 men. His old comrade-in-arms General Ney, who had refused to march on Paris the year before and had urged Napoleon to surrender, now rejoined him. Hearing of Napoleon's triumphant return, Louis XVIII fled the capital in fright. When Napoleon arrived on March 20, Paris was waiting for him, just as he had predicted to his soldiers. He had been gone for only 10 months.

However, the allies were waiting for him too and immediately planned for war. Once again their armies began to close in on France from all sides. The British and Prussians were massing their troops to the north, in Belgium. Napoleon decided to face them first. Then he would turn eastward to deal with the Austrians and Russians.

He managed to raise an army of 128,000 men and 344 guns. The size of the opposing army in Belgium alone was 200,000 men and 500 guns. Nevertheless, he went on the attack and took his stand at a place called Waterloo.

The commander of the allied forces was the duke of Wellington, who had beaten the French in the Peninsular War. Napoleon's old generals who had served in Spain had a healthy respect for Wellington, but Napoleon mocked them: "Because you have been beaten by Wellington, you consider him a great general. And I tell you that Wellington is a bad general, that the English are bad soldiers, and that the whole thing will be a walkover. . . . We shall sleep in Brussels tonight."

On June 18, 1815, with 30,000 of his men off on a wild goose chase after the Prussians, Napoleon faced Wellington at Waterloo. The battle raged for hours, and Napoleon seemed on the verge of victory. "I've got them," he shouted. "They're ours." Then the Prussians showed up to relieve Wellington, while the 30,000 French reinforcements never arrived. By nightfall Napoleon had gone down to defeat. A broken man, he raced back to Paris in tears. His return to power—the Hundred Days—was over.

The Battle of Waterloo is one of the most studied

**A caricature of Napoleon's escape from Elba on February 26, 1815. After 10 months in exile, he slipped past his guards and set sail with an army of 1,000 men, hoping to make a triumphal return to France.**

Napoleon at Waterloo, June 18, 1815. Greatly outnumbered, his troops fought valiantly in the last battle of Napoleon's life but were routed by the arrival of Prussian reinforcements.

battles in history, and there are numerous theories as to why Napoleon lost. For one thing, the duke of Wellington was a remarkable strategist who possessed much courage, good sense, and willpower. For another, he had excellent field positions and more troops than Napoleon. But even he called Waterloo "a damned nice thing," which is the British way of saying that it was a close call.

Napoleon left his throne for the last time on June 22, 1815. He decided to sail for America and start a new life, but he was intercepted by the British. This time they wanted to make sure that he would be out of the way for good.

In October 1815 Napoleon disembarked from a British ship at St. Helena, a speck of an island in the middle of the South Atlantic, thousands of miles from the nearest continent. He spent the rest of his life there, alone except for a few devoted followers. Josephine had died in 1814. Marie Louise

had taken to her heels during the first abdication crisis. She returned to Austria with Napoleon's beloved son and heir, François-Charles-Joseph, who had a short and unhappy life. Back at home she

Aboard the *Bellerophon*, the ship that took him to permanent exile on the remote South Atlantic island of St. Helena, British naval officers watch Napoleon with an understandable mixture of suspicion and awe.

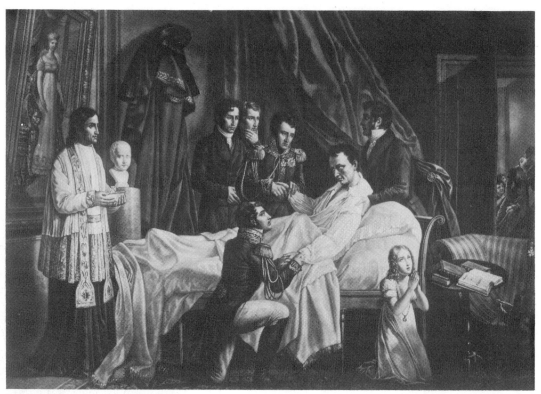

**Napoleon on his deathbed, as portrayed by Vernet. He died on May 5, 1821. In his will he requested that he be laid to rest along the banks of the Seine, but he was buried on St. Helena. His remains were returned to a place of honor in Paris in 1840, during the reign of King Louis-Philippe (1773–1850).**

quickly forgot Napoleon and started an affair with an Austrian count.

When Napoleon learned that he was to be stripped of his title and exiled to St. Helena, he had protested, "I appeal to history!" On St. Helena he devoted himself to laying the groundwork for that appeal. He dictated his memoirs and spent long hours justifying his every action. As always, he was his own best propagandist.

Napoleon also kept up a running battle with the British governor of the island, who refused to deliver packages addressed to "Emperor Napoleon" and generally made life difficult for his prisoner. In his will, Napoleon wrote:

"I wish my ashes to rest on the banks of the Seine, in the midst of that French people which I have loved so much. . . . I die before my time, killed by the English oligarchy and its hired assassins."

On May 5, 1821, at the age of 51, Napoleon died. He was buried on St. Helena. Until recently it was thought that he died of cancer of the stomach, as had two of his sisters and his father. But there is now another theory.

Some years ago a Swedish dentist named Sten Forshufvud became intrigued by a description of Napoleon's last days on St. Helena. He began to suspect that the former emperor had died of arsenic poisoning. A chemical analysis of Napoleon's hair confirmed his notion.

After long study and a careful reading of the diaries of everyone close to Napoleon, Forshufvud and another Napoleon expert, Ben Weider, concluded that Napoleon was slowly murdered by Count Charles-Tristan de Montholon. He was probably hired by the count of Artois, a Bourbon prince who became King Charles X in 1824.

The Bourbons were terrified that Napoleon might escape from St. Helena as he had from Elba and try to overthrow them. If they had him assassinated the French people might find out and rise up against them. Slow arsenic poisoning was almost foolproof. Though it might take years, Napoleon would be too ill to cause trouble.

Once the poison had damaged his body, the murderers could count on the doctors giving him the final blow. At the time arsenic poisoning was often mistaken for other illnesses. The recommended treatment for these illnesses was a massive dose of calomel. Calomel did two things for victims of arsenic poisoning. First it killed them, and then it cleared the system of all traces of arsenic.

Napoleon was not embalmed before his burial. In 1840 his body was returned to France according to his wishes and given a final resting place of honor in Paris. When the coffin was opened, everyone expected to see nothing but a skeleton. Instead the body was perfectly preserved after 20 years! This is another side effect of arsenic, which acts as a preservative. It is often used for museum and laboratory specimens. Napoleon was thus able to testify to his murder from the grave.

The story of Napoleon is the story of the meteoric rise and fall of one man born on a small island with few advantages other than his brains, his

King Charles X of France (1757–1836). Known as the count of Artois before he assumed the throne, he was the leader of the *emigré* opposition to Napoleon. It has been suggested that Napoleon died from arsenic poisoning at the hands of a trusted aide secretly in the count's pay.

willpower, and his imagination. It is also the story of revolution, of the change from the old order to the modern world. Scholars are still debating Napoleon's qualities as a leader and his impact on history. Some stress his magnetism, his charm, his enormous energy and industry; others emphasize his arrogance, egotism, and contempt for human life. Some consider him the enlightened bearer of revolutionary ideals; others regard him as a forerunner of 20th-century dictators.

It is hard to assess his role. He redrew the map of Europe several times. He brought lasting reforms to the legal, administrative, judicial, and educational systems of an entire continent. He revolutionized warfare. But the political and social upheavals, such as the French Revolution, that shook France and the rest of Europe would have happened without him.

Many of his actions brought unintended results. He paved the way for the unification of Italy and Germany. He helped make the United States a world power by selling the Louisiana Territory. His war with Spain gave the countries of Latin America an opportunity to fight for their independence. He strengthened the pope and the Catholic church despite all his attempts to do the opposite.

Napoleon left behind a powerful legend that grew to enormous proportions after his death. His son, Napoleon II, never ruled France. But in 1852 his nephew, Louis Napoleon, traded on the popularity of his name to proclaim the Second Empire, and took the title Napoleon III. Bonapartism—the belief in a strong, authoritarian ruler appointed by the will of the people—continued to cast its spell over French politics for years and remains a tangible force even today.

Napoleon has inspired literally hundreds of thousands of books. Legions of paintings, poems, plays, and films celebrate his deeds. Whatever his precise historical role, he was an enormously forceful personality, a figure larger than life. Whether we admire him or hate him, praise him or damn him, it is hard to disagree with his own remark about himself: "What a novel my life has been!"

Napoleon's death mask. His coffin was opened when his body was returned to France in 1840, and after 20 years his face was hardly changed—a fact that lends strong support to the poisoning theory, since arsenic is a highly effective preservative.

The hat, pants, and vest worn by Napoleon on St. Helena. A portrait of the former emperor dictating his memoirs hangs on the wall in the background.

# ─────────── Further Reading ───────────

Albrecht-Carrié, René. *Europe 1500–1848*. Paterson, New Jersey: Littlefield, Adams and Co., 1962.

Barnett, Correlli. *Bonaparte*. New York: Hill and Wang, 1978.

Butterfield, Herbert. *Napoleon*. New York: Macmillan Publishing Co., Inc., 1962.

Castelot, André. *Napoleon*. New York: Harper and Row, 1971.

de Chair, Somerset, ed. *Napoleon's Memoirs*. New York: Harper Brothers, 1949.

Herold, J. Christopher. *The Age of Napoleon*. New York: American Heritage Publishing Co., Inc., 1983.

Korngold, Ralph. *The Last Years of Napoleon*. New York: Harcourt, Brace and Co., 1959.

Weider, Ben and David Hapgood. *The Murder of Napoleon*. New York: Berkley Publishing Corp., 1983.

# Chronology

| | |
|---|---|
| Aug. 15, 1769 | Born in Ajaccio, Corsica |
| April 1779 | Commences military schooling at Brienne |
| Oct. 1784 | Transfers to Ecole Militaire, Paris |
| 1785 | Assigned to artillery regiment at Valence |
| 1789 | The French Revolution commences |
| 1793 | Napoleon promoted brigadier general |
| Feb. 1794 | Assigned to senior command with France's Army of Italy |
| Oct. 1795 | Defends Convention against royalist uprising |
| March 9, 1796 | Marries Josephine de Beauharnais |
| 1796—97 | Campaigns in Italy |
| Oct. 17, 1797 | Concludes Treaty of Campo-Formio |
| 1798—99 | Campaigns in Egypt |
| Nov. 10, 1799 | Overthrows Directory and establishes Consulate |
| Feb. 7, 1800 | Becomes First Consul |
| June 14, 1800 | Defeats Austrian armies at Marengo |
| July 15, 1801 | Concludes negotiation of Concordat with Roman Catholic church |
| Aug. 15, 1802 | Appointed First Consul for life |
| May 1804 | Proclaimed emperor of France |
| 1805 | Assumes title of king of Italy |
| | Leads French armies against Third Coalition and achieves decisive victory at Austerlitz |
| Oct. 14, 1806 | Defeats Prussians at Jena and Auerstädt |
| June 14, 1807 | Defeats Russians at Friedland |
| July 7, 1807 | Negotiates Treaty of Tilsit with Tsar Alexander I |
| Dec. 1809 | Divorces Josephine |
| April 1810 | Marries Archduchess Marie Louise of Austria |
| June 22, 1812 | Napoleon's armies invade Russia |
| Sept. 7, 1812 | Inconclusive battle fought at Borodino |
| Sept. 14, 1812 | Napoleon's armies enter Moscow |
| Oct. 1812 | Napoleon orders retreat from Moscow |
| Oct. 19, 1813 | Defeated at Leipzig by combined armies of Russia, Prussia, and Austria |
| April 6, 1814 | Abdicates |
| Feb. 26, 1815 | Escapes from Elba and proclaims himself emperor |
| June 18, 1815 | Suffers decisive defeat at Waterloo |
| June 22, 1815 | Relinquishes imperial powers for the last time |
| May 5, 1821 | Dies, probably of arsenic poisoning, on St. Helena |

# Index

**Leslie McGuire** is a writer and editor living in New York City. A graduate of Barnard College, she was a contributing editor to The Concise Columbia Encyclopedia, and has written many books for children.

**Arthur M. Schlesinger, jr.,** taught history at Harvard for many years and is currently Albert Schweitzer Professor of the Humanities at City University of New York. He is the author of numerous highly praised works in American history and has twice been awarded the Pulitzer Prize. He served in the White House as special assistant to presidents Kennedy and Johnson.